STUDIES
of
FAMILIAR
HYMNS
By
LOUIS F. BENSON, D.D.

SECOND SERIES

THE REV. GEORGE WHITEFIELD

STUDIES

OF

FAMILIAR HYMNS

SECOND SERIES

BY

LOUIS F. BENSON, D.D.

EDITOR OF "THE HYMNAL PUBLISHED IN 1895 AND REVISED IN
1911 BY AUTHORITY OF THE GENERAL ASSEMBLY OF THE
PRESBYTERIAN CHURCH IN THE U.S.A.," AND
AUTHOR OF "THE ENGLISH HYMN"

PHILADELPHIA
THE WESTMINSTER PRESS
1926

COPYRIGHT, 1923, BY THE

BOARD OF CHRISTIAN EDUCATION OF THE

PRESBYTERIAN CHURCH IN THE U.S.A.

Published November, 1923
Reprinted, October, 1926

PRINTED IN THE UNITED STATES OF AMERICA

PREFACE

Twenty years have passed since the appearance of an earlier series of *Studies of Familiar Hymns*. They had been running through the numbers of " Forward," the young people's paper of the Presbyterian Church, and in 1903 were gathered into a volume. The reception of the book was kindly — kindly enough at least to make plain that a considerable number of people, who wished information concerning the hymns they loved, were willing to forego the primrose paths of dalliance with myths and misstatements, anecdotage and sentimentalism, and to be personally conducted along the straiter and less flowery paths of truth.

The number of these stout hearts does not appear to diminish. It was indeed the author's discovery that after so many years the demand for his little book continues, and is indeed larger now than at first, which has encouraged him to invite his readers, old and new, to accompany him a little farther afield.

In motive and in method the new Studies are very like the old, even to the appending to each of " Some Points for Discussion " in " the hope (now renewed) that groups or societies of young people might be led to think over and discuss the message of the hymns they so often sing, sometimes, it may be, too thoughtlessly."

There are, however, between the earlier Studies and these two points of difference to which an old reader's attention may well be called.

First. In making such studies it is necessary (now as then) to have some standard, common to author and reader, not only for the text of the hymns dealt with but also in allusions to other hymns. In the earlier book the standard was *The Hymnal published by authority of the General Assembly of the Presbyterian Church in the U. S. A.* in 1895. Since then it has been followed by *The Hymnal . . . revised in 1911.* In the present volume accordingly the Revision of 1911 becomes the standard. The author wishes he could alter the plates of the earlier Studies so as to make all references to hymns there conform with those in this book. But in view of the great number of copies of *The Hymnal* of 1895 still in actual use in the churches, and for other reasons, this change is not now practicable.

Second. In the earlier series there was no intended connection between the hymns studied — no continued story: each of them being chosen for its own sake and with an eye upon the author's ability to furnish an autographed copy of the hymn by way of illustration. The plan of the present series is more ambitious — there *is* a continued story. The hymns, with one exception that will explain itself, are arranged in chronological order, and were chosen as representative of the historical development of hymnody and of hymn singing among the peoples of England, Scotland, and America.

The story begins with the joy and pride of English-speaking Christians in their new-found privilege of singing God's praise in their own tongue, although with the restriction (suggested by John Calvin) that they should confine their praises to the very words of Scripture. It recounts the fading of the joy out of the Psalmody, and the growth of dissatisfaction with the restriction.

It celebrates the advance of a young champion (Isaac Watts) to attack single-handed the authority and tradition of "Bible-Songs," and tells how the great eighteenth century revival brought about the final vindication of the people's right to express their praises in terms of their own experience rather than that of "David." It goes forward to narrate how the spiritual forces of the nineteenth century dealt with "the hymn of human composure" it had inherited from the great revival; and attempts to set some of our modern hymns, one by one, against the background of that particular epoch or phase of religious history out of which each hymn came in its turn, and which so often explains the content and even the form of the hymn.

In the preparation of these Studies the great aim of the author has been the attainment of a scrupulous accuracy in smaller as in larger things; his great pleasure has been in the atmosphere of friendship with which that preparation was surrounded. His outspoken thanks are due to the Reverend Doctor John T. Faris, who enlarged his editorial heart to make room in "Forward" for so long a series of long papers; to his associate, the Reverend Park Hays Miller, for that sympathetic encouragement which makes the sunny side of honest work; to Miss Anné Henderson, who read all these Studies in manuscript more than once (could kindness farther go?) to their advantage; and to Mr. Henry F. Scheetz, for his zeal "to make this book [outwardly] better than the last."

NORTHEAST HARBOR, MAINE
September 22, 1923.

ANALYTICAL TABLE OF CONTENTS

xi

LIST OF ILLUSTRATIONS

STUDIES OF FAMILIAR HYMNS

I

ALL PEOPLE THAT ON EARTH DO DWELL

THE TEXT OF THE "PSALM"

1 All people that on earth do dwell,
  Sing to the Lord with cheerful voice,
  Him serve with fear, His praise forth tell,
  Come ye before Him and rejoice.

2 The Lord ye know is God indeed;
  Without our aid He did us make;
  We are His folk, He doth us feed;
  And for His sheep He doth us take.

3 O enter then His gates with praise,
  Approach with joy His courts unto;
  Praise, laud, and bless His Name always,
  For it is seemly so to do.

4 For why? the Lord our God is good,
  His mercy is for ever sure;
  His truth at all times firmly stood,
  And shall from age to age endure.

> The Hundredth Psalm. Translated into English me-
> ter by the Rev. William Kethe, while an Exile at
> Geneva, Switzerland.

NOTE. The text is that printed in the incomplete Metrical Psalter published in London by John Day, 1561; without any changes except for the modernizing of the punctuation and of some old-time spellings.

This version of the Hundredth Psalm, with " The Old Hundredth " Psalm tune that belongs to it, is a real antique. It is like a piece of old English silver plate, more stately and massive than our modern make. The Psalm and tune have been sung together, in England and Scotland and America, for more than three centuries and a half, and would be worth keeping in our hymnals, if only for their associations. For they take us back to the time when our forefathers first began to praise God in His sanctuary in their own English tongue. But in fact they still make a noble hymn of praise. To hear it sung solidly and reverently by a great congregation, with the support of the full organ, is a religious experience. It gives one's faith a fresh grip on the big and holy things that " shall from age to age indure."

THE STORY OF "OLD HUNDRED"

It begins in Geneva. The city of Geneva lies within that part of Switzerland where the people speak French and not German. John Calvin went there in 1536 to help on the Reformation. He was a very shrewd Frenchman, and knew as well as Luther did that the best way to arouse the hearts of the people was to get them to singing religious songs. He asked to be allowed to make a start by having the children taught to sing Psalms in church, till the congregation should get familiar with them and feel moved to join in. But Calvin's rather severe way of looking at things, together no doubt with the uncompromising vigor of his character, very quickly got him disliked both by the rulers and the people. Before any of his plans could be tried out, he was banished.

JOHN CALVIN

Calvin found himself the pastor of a little flock of French Protestant refugees in Strasburg, where all the German Protestants around them were singing the new hymns Luther and his friends had written for them. Calvin took some of the German tunes, set them to a few Bible Psalms and canticles translated into French verse, and printed them in a thin Psalm book for his congregation. But he took none of the German hymns. He was a bit suspicious of hymns. It is so easy, he thought, to slip false doctrines beneath the pretty phrases of poetry, and to lodge them in the singers' hearts. Why not sing the songs God has given us in the Bible, the Psalms, especially? Surely they are the best, true because inspired, and quite as beautiful as any man-made hymns.

When they recalled Calvin to Geneva, one of the conditions of his return was that he should have his own way about singing Psalms in church. And his own way took shape in a somewhat larger Psalm book, with some new versifyings of Psalms by the popular poet, Clément Marot, and some fresh tunes by an excellent French musician whom Calvin got to help him. Our familiar " Old Hundred " is the tune composed by Louis Bourgeois to fit the meter of the One Hundred and Thirty-fourth Psalm, in an enlarged edition of this Genevan Psalm Book printed in 1551. How it became the One Hundredth and not the One Hundredth and Thirty-fourth Psalm tune, we are now to see.

THE STORY OF THE "PSALM"

Switzerland and England were far apart in those days. But Calvin's doctrines and his doings at Geneva

were well known in London. The English Protestants
had come to take Calvin rather than Luther as their
model and leader. When they put together their first
English Prayer Book, their thought had been to depart
as little as might be from the structure and ceremonies
of the Latin Mass Book and Breviary of the old Church.
But the Prayer Book of 1549 was hardly printed before
Cranmer began to make changes of a kind that Calvin
would approve of. And the second Prayer Book of 1552
was a very different book, more Protestant, more Calvinistic even. By that time many were hoping to drop
the Prayer Book altogether, and use the simpler services
Calvin had prepared for Geneva. They had already
begun to sing metrical Psalms in church after Calvin's
model — an innovation in which the Chapel Royal itself
took the lead. Just then the boy king, Edward VI, died.
The Roman Catholic Queen Mary came to the throne,
and many of the Protestants fled the country.

A little company of these exiles, of the sort soon to
be called Puritans, settled at Frankfort. There they
felt free to simplify their worship. But they were soon
joined by another party of more churchly proclivities,
who insisted that the full Prayer Book services be
reinstated. That led to the historic " Troubles at
Frankfort." The Puritan party left, and went to Geneva to be under the wing of Calvin. There they formed
an English church, with the Scotchman, John Knox,
as one of its pastors.

The Englishmen were deeply moved by the sight of
Calvin's great congregation in the old cathedral, with
their little Psalm books in their own hands, by the
great volume of voices praising God in their own French
tongue, and by the beautiful melodies carrying the words,

by the fervor of the singing and the spiritual uplift of the singers. The English exiles felt that their ideals of pure worship were realized, and had a vision of the cathedrals and parish churches at home, freed of " the last dregs of popery " and filled with the sound of many voices praising God in the holy songs He had put into their mouths.

They had with them a few Psalms that had been versified at home, and now they proceeded to prepare an English Psalm Book with tunes in it, just like Calvin's. There were scholars among them who could translate Psalms from the original Hebrew and several who could turn the translations into respectable English verse. The tunes were their greatest bother, because the meters of the tunes the Genevans were singing would be awkward to Englishmen. There was one tune, however, that to the One Hundred and Thirty-fourth Psalm, in what we call " long meter," that seemed available and was certainly beautiful. And for its sake one of the exiles, William Kethe, chose the Hundredth Psalm to translate into that meter. And the words of his Psalm, " All people that on earth do dwell," were then and there married to Bourgeois' tune in a union so close and so lasting that it is hard to say which is " The Old Hundredth."

Queen Mary's reign was happily as short as Edward's, and the exiles did not stay at Geneva long enough to complete their Psalm Book. Kethe's Psalm appeared in their last edition, containing eighty-seven Psalms. That was printed in 1561, and by that time most of the exiles had come home. The complete edition of the English Psalter was prepared at London, printed there in 1562. It was called *The whole Booke of Psalms, col-*

Aaron le Prestre de la Loy.

2 Et qui depuis la teste vient descendre
Iusqu'à la barbe,& en fin se vient rendre
Aux bords du sacré vestement:
Comme l'humeur se voit iournellement,
Du mont Hermon,& Sion decourir,
Et le pays d'embas nourrir:
3 Ainsi pour vray ceste assemblee heureuse
Sent du Seigneur la faueur plantureuse,
Voire pour iamais ne mourir.

Ecce,nunc benedicite. PSE. CXXXIIII. T. DE BE.

Il admoneste les Leuites de faire leur deuoir, les asseurant de la faueur de Dieu.

1 OR sus, seruiteurs du Seigneur, Vous
qui de nuit en son honneur Dedans sa maison
le seruez,Louëz-le,& son nom esleuez.

2 Leuez les mains au plus saint lieu
De ce tres-saint temple de Dieu,
Et le los qu'il a merité
Soit par vos bouches recité.
3 Dieu qui a fait & entretient,
Et terre & ciel par son pouuoir,

V

lected into English metre, but is familiarly known as
" Sternhold and Hopkins."

A strange thing is that Kethe's Hundredth Psalm
was not in it. A less attractive version took its place.
Kethe's first appeared again in an appendix of 1564 and
in its proper place the following year. How that happened we shall never know.

The Puritan exiles' dream of a Church of England in
which Calvin's Genevan order of worship should re-
place the Prayer Book, was never to be realized. But
they did succeed in rooting firmly on English soil the
Calvinistic ideal and practice of having the congregation's praise confined to the songs of Scripture. The
Prayer Book and the Psalm Book flourished side by
side. The curious result of this arrangement was to
provide the Church of England with a double system
of Psalmody, — the prose Psalms already in the Prayer
Book, and now its metrical Psalms in the Psalm Book.
But there were no hymn books in the pews till after
the Evangelical Revival of the eighteenth century.

THE AUTHOR OF THE "PSALM"

As to the author of the Hundredth Psalm itself,
the Bible gives us no information. As to William
Kethe, who made this English version, we know very
little. We do not know what he did in Edward VI's
time. The old authorities call him a Scotchman. We
know he was one of those who exiled themselves to
escape the attentions of bloody Mary. He was one
of the English congregation of rather radical Protestants
at Frankfort, and left there to go with them to
Geneva, where he became prominent in the English

Church. He was nearer to being a poet than were any of his colleagues, and contributed twenty-four versions to the exiles' Psalm Book. Besides his Psalms he wrote poems and religious ballads: his " Tye thy mare, Tom boye " becoming quite noted. He helped also in the translation of the Bible, which was another achievement of the English exiles at Geneva. When he went home he was made rector of a church in Dorset, and was chaplain to the English troops in an expedition to Havre and in a later campaign against Popish rebels in the north. The preaching of a sermon in 1571 is the latest record we have of Kethe's life, though it may have continued till the appointment in 1608 of a successor in his Dorset rectorate.

SOME POINTS FOR DISCUSSION

1. The English Metrical Psalms were printed complete about two years before Shakespeare was born, in April, 1564. The Psalm Book seems to have been used in the homes as a religious primer as well as at church. At any rate, the people in Shakespeare's time were required by law to go to church regularly, and he became very familiar with the Metrical Psalms. He quotes from the Psalm Book several times. Indeed if we are to follow the modern text of his plays, he singles out this Hundredth Psalm for mention in *The Merry Wives of Windsor* (Act II, scene i), speaking of the awkwardness of singing " The Hundredth Psalm to the tune of ' Green Sleeves.' " And we are at liberty to conclude that Shakespeare was especially impressed by the singing of the Hundredth Psalm to the familiar tune. But the old texts of the play do not read " the Hun-

dredth Psalm," but " the hundred psalms." The present
writer has given elsewhere * his reasons for thinking the
old text correct, and that it refers to the title of a book
printed at London in 1561 for the Dutch and Flemish
refugees in England, and called *Hondert Psalmen
Dauids*. The predilection of these foreigners for Psalm
singing is noticed by Shakespeare more than once.

In Longfellow's *The Courtship of Miles Standish* there
is also a reference to the Hundredth Psalm in metre,
when John Alden heard

" the musical voice of Priscilla
Singing the hundredth Psalm, the grand old Puritan anthem,
Music that Luther sang to the sacred words of the Psalmist."

The reference here is to the tune " Old Hundred," under
the supposition that it was one of the Lutheran chorales.
But the words Priscilla sang were from Henry Ains-
worth's version of the Psalm in his *The Book of Psalms:
Englished both in prose and metre*. This was printed
in Amsterdam in 1612, and was the Psalm Book the
Pilgrim fathers brought to Plymouth.

2. Like the lettering on an ancient stone, the text of
Kethe's Psalm is read differently by different people.
The first to give a new reading was an early printer
of the Metrical Psalms who mistook the word " folck "
(folk, people) in line seven. He printed it " flock " and
was followed by later printers of the Psalm Book and
by most modern hymn books. In the Scottish Psalm
Book " Him serve with fear " is changed to " Him
serve with mirth," and " The Lord ye know " to " Know
that the Lord." Are such changes worth while? *The
Hymnal* text is an attempt to print the original without

* In the *Journal of the Presbyterian Historical Society* for
June, 1918.

change except for the ancient spellings such as " yt "
for " that," " ye " for " the," " shep " for " sheep,"
" indure " for " endure." It is a puzzle whether we
should retain the question mark after " For why? " as
it means simply " because." But why not? We like an
antique for its very quaintness.

3. The melodies Calvin had prepared for his Psalm
Book are very lovely. But it has not proved easy to
bring them back into use. " St. Michael " and " Autumn " in *The Hymnal* are arranged from Genevan
melodies, but these have been subjected to rough treatment. The facsimile will show how we have changed
the rhythm and movement even of " Old Hundred "
by making all the notes of equal length. We have done
it to our loss, many musicians think, and they are anxious to have the tune restored to its original beauty.

II

THE LORD'S MY SHEPHERD, I'LL NOT WANT

THE TEXT OF THE "PSALM."

1 The Lord's my Shepherd, I'll not want;
  He makes me down to lie
In pastures green, He leadeth me
  The quiet waters by.

2 My soul He doth restore again;
  And me to walk doth make
Within the paths of righteousness,
  Ev'n for His own Name's sake.

3 Yea, though I walk in death's dark vale,
  Yet will I fear none ill;
For thou art with me, and Thy rod
  And staff me comfort still.

4 My table Thou hast furnishèd
  In presence of my foes;
My head Thou dost with oil anoint,
  And my cup overflows.

5 Goodness and mercy all my life
  Shall surely follow me;
And in God's house for evermore
  My dwelling-place shall be.

The Twenty-third Psalm in meter, as approved by the
General Assembly of the Church of Scotland in 1649:
based on versions by Francis Rous, Sir William
Mure, and others.

12

NOTE. The text (apart from a few spellings) is the original text of *The Psalms of David in meeter,* 1650, with the exception of the seventh line. In the writer's copy that line begins with " Into " and not " Within." The alteration was made at an early date, perhaps for euphony's sake, and " Within " became the accepted reading of the authorized editions of *The Psalms in meeter.*

THE PSALM THAT " NEVER RUNS DRY "

The Hundredth Psalm, treated in our first study, was one of the songs of the English Reformation. This version of the Twenty-third is of Oliver Cromwell's time, and is altogether Scottish and Presbyterian in its origin, its use, and its associations. It is one of *The Psalms of David in meeter* adopted by the Church of Scotland in 1649, commonly called " Rous's Version " or " Rous " for short. Its real story can never be written. It was spelled out in the religious experiences of the most self-contained people on earth, the Scots.

The story begins with the printing of the Psalms in meter at the end of the Scottish Bibles, in a day when there were very few books in the cottages, and the singing of them twice a day at family worship as well as at church. Gradually the Psalms in meter became, even more than the prose Bible Psalms, the special word of God to His people in Scotland on every occasion of their lives, and especially in their times of trouble. There were Psalms that appealed to the dour side of the Scot and roused and sustained his combative instincts. But there was also a side of real tenderness in the Scottish heart; and this Twenty-third Psalm in meter, most of all, touched it and brought it peace.

Word by word, every line of this Psalm was engraved on the memory and clasped to the heart of generation after generation of loyal Scots. It was a home song, first of all, learned at the mother's knee, a household word; and then, as the children grew up and went out of the old home, a possession, or rather a part of their inmost selves, that went with them wherever they traveled or found new homes; an inward vision of pastures green, a rod and staff of comfort on the way, and at the end a light in death's dark vale.

It would not be difficult to collect incidents testifying to the intense feeling of the Scots for their *Psalms in meeter*, and for this Twenty-third Psalm in particular. Better still for such a purpose is a story of Ian Maclaren, who understood so well the heart of his countrymen. It is the story of an old Scot, hard and rugged, but laid low at last on one of the beds of an English hospital ward. He had just been told that he would die at break of day, but he had declined the ministrations of the chaplain, an Episcopalian. " He micht want to read a prayer, and a' cudna abide that."

In the afternoon a good lady who had heard of the old man's loneliness came to his bedside and asked if she might not sing some comforting hymn, opening the book to find " Rock of Ages." He shook his head.

" Ye're verra kind, mem, and a'm muckle obleeged to ye, but a'm a Scot and ye're English, and ye dinna understand. A' my days hev I been protestin' against the use o' human hymns in the praise o' God; a've left three kirks on that account, and raised my testimony in public places, and noo wud ye send me into eternity wi' the sough o' hymn in my ears?

" Ye'll excuse me, mem, for a'm no ungratefu'," he continued, " and I wud like to meet yir wishes when ye've been so kind to me. The doctor says I canna live

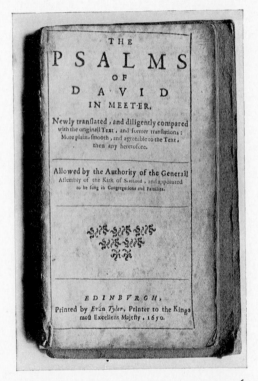

THE

PSALMS

OF

DAVID

IN MEETER.

Newly tranſlated, and diligently compared
with the originall Text, and former tranſlations:
More plain, ſmooth, and agreeable to the Text,
then any heretofore.

Allowed by the Authority of the Generall
Aſſembly of the Kirk of Scotland, and appointed
to be ſung in Congregations and Families.

EDINBVRGH,
Printed by Evan Tyler, Printer to the Kings
moſt Excellent Majeſty, 1650.

TITLE-PAGE OF THE SCOTTISH PSALMS OF 1650

long, and it's possible that my strength may sune give way, but a'll tell ye what a'm willin' to do.

"Sae lang as a've got strength and my reason continues clear, a'm prepared to argue with you concerning the lawfulness of using onything except the Psalms o' David in the praise o' God either in public or in private."

"No, no," the lady said, " I did not know the feeling of the Scots about hymns. But I have been in the Highlands, and learned to love your Psalms. I have some in my book here."

"Div ye think that ye cud sing the Twenty-third Psalm —

"'The Lord's my Shepherd, a'll not want'?

for I wud count it verra comfortin.'"

"Yes," she said, " I can, and I think I love that Psalm more than any hymn."

"It never runs dry," murmured the Scot.

So she sang it from beginning to end slowly and reverently, as she had heard it in Scotland. He joined in no word, but ever he kept time with his hand; and, after she ceased, " Thank ye, thank ye," he said, and then both were silent for a few minutes, because she saw that he was in his own country, and did not wish to bring him back.

"Mem, ye've dune me the greatest kindness ony Christian cud do for anither as he stands on the banks of the Jordan."

For a minute he was silent again, and then he said:

"A'm gaein' to tell ye somethin', and I think ye'll understand. Ma wife and me wes married thirty-five years, and ilka nicht of oor married life we sang a Psalm afore we gaed to rest. She took the air and a' took the bass, and we sang the Psalms through frae beginning to end twal times. She was taken frae me ten year ago, and the nicht afore she dee'd we sang the Twenty-third Psalm. A've never sung the Psalm since, and a' didna join wi' ye when ye sang it, for a'm waitin' to sing it wi' her noo in oor Father's hoose the mornin's mornin', where there'll be nae nicht nor partin' evermore."

THE STORY OF ROUS'S VERSION

We spoke in the first study of the little church of English exiles in Queen Mary's time at Geneva, with John Knox as pastor, and of the English Psalm Book which they worked at and carried home to England, where it was completed in 1562. When Knox went home to Scotland he also took that Psalm Book, and there it was completed in much the same way, and printed in 1564. And so the Episcopalians in England and the Presbyterians in Scotland became Psalm singers in Calvin's fashion.

The Scots kept on using the old Psalm Book for nearly a century. That brings us down to the effort of Charles I to turn the Church of Scotland into an episcopal Church, and the outbreak of the Civil War in 1639. Charles needed money to suppress the Scots, and had to call a Parliament to provide it. But the Parliament, mostly Puritans, declared war on Charles himself; and to secure the aid of the Scots, united with them in the Solemn League and Covenant of 1643, to preserve the Presbyterian Church in Scotland and to set it up in England and Ireland. Then it was that the famous Westminster Assembly was called, to prepare common standards of faith and worship for the three kingdoms. It was agreed on all hands that the churches should sing

Psalms and not hymns. But what version of the Psalms? The Assembly recommended the Parliament to adopt a new version made by one of its own members, Francis Rous.

He was an English gentleman of much distinction, a Calvinist by conviction, a believer in the Presbyterian system, and several times a member of Parliament. He was sent to the Westminster Assembly as a lay commissioner, and was afterward Provost of Eton College. He made his metrical version of the Psalms in hope of meeting the widespread demand among the Puritans of the time for a more exact and literal rendering than that contained in the old Psalm Books of England and Scotland.

It seems a bit odd to us, who take such things lightly enough, that Parliament should wrangle over the particular version of the Psalms to be used in church. It did not seem so then. The House of Commons agreed to adopt Rous's Version and ordered that it and none other be sung in all the churches of the Kingdom. But a rival of Rous, one William Barton, had many friends in the House of Lords, who put up a stiff fight for his version, and when the Commons' adoption of Rous came there for concurrent action, they succeeded in shelving it by having it referred to a committee.

It did not matter much, for this first " Presbyterian Alliance " was soon to be broken up. The Church of Scotland, left alone again, adopted the standards of the Westminster Assembly, but hesitated about the Psalm Book. Finally, after three years of debating and tinkering, they adopted Rous's Version, though it had been so much altered and added to that it hardly deserved to bear his name. Such as it was, it continued to be the

FRANCIS ROUS, 1656

only praise book of the Church of Scotland until recent times, when the right to sing " hymns of human composure " has been won after bitter struggles. " Rous " was brought to this country also by the Scotch and Irish immigrants, and was the chief Psalm Book of the Presbyterian Churches in America.

SOME POINTS FOR DISCUSSION

1. Seventeen Presbyterian or Reformed denominations in various countries, some of them very small, still confine their praise to Bible Psalms and reject human hymns. So " the subject matter of praise " must still be a topic for discussion. These denominations seem to agree that God intended the Book of Psalms to be the only praise book of His Church until the end of time. As lately as 1905, two conventions were held under the direction of the General Assembly of the United Presbyterian Church of North America, " to promote the claims of the Psalms in the field of worship." And the papers at these gatherings have been printed in an imposing volume. It is doubtful, however, whether the cause was materially advanced by these means, or whether in the minds of the great majority of Christians the old issue of Psalm *versus* Hymn is either alive or capable of revival.

2. There are four versions of the Twenty-third Psalm in *The Hymnal revised*.

The first is the one we are now discussing. Those who have inherited Scottish blood and traditions very likely feel that it has passed beyond the pale of criticism.

The second, " The Lord my pasture shall prepare," was contributed to the famous weekly, *The Spectator*, by the Right Honorable Joseph Addison. He was a de-

lightful writer, and a gentle wind still blows over the
"verdant landscape" of his Psalm. It is quite true,
however, as Canon Douglass has said, that Addison was
a great deal more fond of adjectives than David was.

The third, "The Lord my Shepherd is," one of Dr.
Isaac Watts's versifications, is hardly one of his suc-
cesses. It is so hard and jerky. It was put in *The
Hymnal* to gratify a prominent elder and warm friend
of that book, who had associations with it. But he does
not need it any longer, and the Watts version might
well be allowed to drop out.

The fourth, "The King of love my Shepherd is,"
represents the perfection of what we may call the
modern "art and craft" of hymn-making. "How
beautiful are Thy thoughts unto me, O God!" the writer
seems to be saying, as his pen flows on from verse to
verse of the old Psalm. It is a gospel Psalm to him, with
Christ, the Good Shepherd, holding the cross to guide
him. The Rev. Sir Henry Williams Baker wrote it for
the appendix to his *Hymns ancient and modern*, the
most famous hymnal of recent times. And when he came
to die, the last words that could be distinguished were:

> "And on His shoulder gently laid,
> And home, rejoicing, brought me."

3. In the old days "The Lord's my Shepherd, I'll not
want" was sung to one of the still older Scottish Psalm
tunes, often perhaps to the one they called "French"
and we call "Dundee." In modern days it is set to
"Balerma" as often as to any other; also a Scottish
tune. "Walden," No. 577 in *The Hymnal revised*, was
composed for this Psalm by a Canadian lawyer, and is
well worth trying.

III

THERE IS A LAND OF PURE DELIGHT

THE TEXT OF THE HYMN

1 There is a land of pure delight,
  Where saints immortal reign;
  Infinite day excludes the night,
  And pleasures banish pain.

2 There everlasting spring abides,
  And never-withering flowers;
  Death, like a narrow sea, divides
  This heavenly land from ours.

3 Sweet fields beyond the swelling flood
  Stand dressed in living green;
  So to the Jews old Canaan stood,
  While Jordan rolled between.

4 But timorous mortals start and shrink
  To cross this narrow sea;
  And linger, shivering, on the brink,
  And fear to launch away.

5 O could we make our doubts remove,
  Those gloomy doubts that rise,
  And see the Canaan that we love
  With unbeclouded eyes;

6 Could we but climb where Moses stood,
  And view the landscape o'er,
  Not Jordan's stream, nor death's cold flood,
  Should fright us from the shore.

Rev. Isaac Watts, 1707

NOTE. The text is taken from the first edition of Dr. Watts's
Hymns and Spiritual Songs, London, 1707, without any change.

Isaac Watts was born on July 17, 1674, in that English town of Southampton which many Americans know best as a port for steamships to Europe. If we went ashore we should find a " Watts Memorial Hall " and a statue of him in his gown and bands as a preacher. But it is his sacred songs and not his sermons that have given him his fame. In Southampton he passed his childhood, and there he spent some six weeks of the year before this hymn appeared in his volume of *Hymns and Spiritual Songs* in 1707. He had come back to the old home, weak from sickness and discouraged no doubt, and very likely these verses reveal the turn his thoughts took just then.

The town lies on a swell of land within the fork of the Test and the Itchen rivers. It may well be that the view across the water of the pleasant meadows of Marchwood on the one side, or, on the other, of the lawns of Weston, glowing in the evening sunlight, suggested the lines:

> " Sweet fields beyond the swelling flood
> Stand dressed in living green."

Our poet Longfellow said that until he saw the first verdure of spring on the meadows of southern England, he did not quite appreciate the meaning of " dressed in living green." " There are some of us," said the Rev. J. Brierly, " who can never look upon a green field with the spring sun on it without this hymn coming to us as a whisper from heaven."

" HYMNS AND SPIRITUAL SONGS "

The subjects of our first two studies were versions of Psalms taken directly from the Bible. The subject of this is " a hymn of human composure " taken out of the writer's own heart. And he did more than other men to break down the custom of Psalm singing and to conquer the English prejudice against uninspired hymns.

Tennyson says in one of his poems that

> The old order changeth, yielding place to new;
> And God fulfills himself in many ways,
> Lest one good custom should corrupt the world.

Now we saw in our first study how Calvin, in his zeal for " the Bible only," determined that even the songs of his congregation in Geneva should be taken from inspired Scripture, and so started the custom of Psalm singing. It was a " good custom " for the time. In France and Scotland Psalm singing became the very life of the Reformation. In England there was some opposition to introducing it, but the plain people took it up vigorously, and it soon became an established feature of the church services. So the Psalm Books were bound up with the Prayer Books.

The singing of Psalms went on without change through the whole of Elizabeth's reign, and as long as the Church of England held together. In the great break-up of the Puritan Revolution some of the new sects then formed — the Quakers, for instance — gave up singing altogether. The large body of Independents, or Congregationalists as we should call them, gave up the Prayer Book but hung on to the old Psalm Book. They kept up the custom, but the life had gone out of the Psalmody. One of their young ministers, Isaac Watts, said that the singing of God's praise is the part of worship nighest heaven, and its performance among themselves the worst on earth. The Psalms were read

out, one line at a time, by a " clerk," and then the congregation sang that line and waited for the next. Very
few tunes were used, and these were drawled out in pro-
longed notes. " To see the dull indifference, the negligent
and thoughtless air that sits upon the faces of a whole
assembly while the Psalm is on their lips, might tempt
even a charitable observer," Watts wrote, " to suspect
the fervency of inward religion."

By the beginning of the eighteenth century the Psalm
singing in the Independent meeting-houses was so distressing that many of the pastors were in consultation
upon the situation. Watts, the youngest and bravest
of them, had his own view of the root of the trouble
and the remedy. The trouble, he thought, grew out
of confining the praise to Psalms, many of which were
inappropriate to our circumstances, and all were on a
lower plane of revelation than the gospel. " We preach
the gospel and pray in Christ's name, and then check
the aroused devotions of Christians by giving out a song
of the old dispensation."

The remedy he proposed was twofold. First, a new
and free translation of the Psalms written in the way
David would have written them if he had been a fully
instructed Christian living in the eighteenth century.
And this scheme Dr. Watts ultimately carried out in 1719
by publishing his *The Psalms of David imitated in the
language of the New Testament, and apply'd to the Christian state and worship.* This book served as a bridge
over the chasm between the Old Testament Psalms and
the evangelical hymns, by which many congregations
passed over without fully perceiving just where they
were going.

The other feature of Watts's proposed remedy was

HYMNS

AND

Spiritual Songs.

In Three BOOKS.

I. Collected from the Scriptures.
II. Compos'd on Divine Subjects.
III. Prepared for the Lord's Supper.

With an ESSAY

Towards the Improvement of Christian Pſalmody, by the Uſe of Evangelical Hymns in Worſhip, as well as the Pſalms of *David*.

By *I. WATTS.*

And they ſung a new Song, ſaying, Thou art worthy, &c. for thou waſt ſlain and haſt redeemed us, &c. Rev. 5. 9.
Soliti eſſent (*i. e. Chriſtiani*) convenire, carmenque Chriſto quaſi Deo dicere. *Plinius* in *Epiſt.*

LONDON,
Printed by *J. Humfreys,* for *John Lawrence,*
at the Angel in the *Poultrey.* 1707.

TITLE-PAGE OF THE FIRST EDITION OF WATTS'S HYMNS

the introduction of evangelical hymns, freely written under the inspirations of the gospel and expressing all the riches that are in Christ. And this he was prepared to apply at once. He had ready, and printed in 1707, more than two hundred of his own in a volume whose full title can be read in the facsimile here given. The essay to which it refers was a rather cruel attack on the principles and prejudices of the Psalm singers, and a vindication of hymns. We have just the same right, he asserted, to compose and sing spiritual songs as to compose and utter original prayers. The Bible is God's word to us. Our songs ought to be our word to God.

Whoever attacks an old religious custom or prejudice must expect to make enemies. And Watts made many. They spoke of his hymns as " Watts's whims." But he touched the hearts of the people, and one by one the Independent congregations came under the spell of the new hymns. We can scarcely appreciate all they meant to people who had never been allowed to utter the name of their Saviour in praise. Dr. Doddridge tells of giving out " Give me the wings of faith to rise " to a village congregation. Tears came to many eyes; some were quite unable to sing at all, and the clerk said he could hardly speak the words, as he lined them out. When something was said after service as to a possible visit from Dr. Watts, one of the company exclaimed, " The very sight of him would be as good as an ordinance to me! "

This popularity of the hymns is said to explain why so few copies of the earlier editions of *Hymns and Spiritual Songs* have survived to our time: the theory being that the great majority of copies were actually thumbed out of existence by rude but affectionate hands.

THE AUTHOR OF THE HYMN

" Before her stood not an Antinous or an Adonis, not even a moderately presentable Englishman, but a minute, sallow-faced anatomy with hook nose, prominent cheek bones, heavy countenance, cadaverous complexion and small eyes." So it is that the latest biographer of Watts describes him in the act of proposing to the beautiful Elizabeth Singer somewhere about 1706. That Miss Singer had formed a high conception of Watts from his poems we know, and that his appearance disappointed her we may assume. But how does the biographer know that Miss Singer in rejecting him said, " Mr. Watts, I only wish I could say that I admire the casket as much as I admire the jewel " ?

It is more to the point to remember that the aging face, beneath its monstrous wig, that has come down to us in the portraits may truly represent the famous and venerated Dr. Watts, but not the somewhat headstrong young man who wrote the hymns with the ardor of youth, and gave battle to the Psalm singers with that self-confidence and disregard of other people's opinions of which perhaps only youth is capable.

The household at Southampton was religious, and the boy's thoughts were serious. " Fell under considerable conviction of sin, 1688, and was taught to trust in Christ, I hope, 1689; " so his diary reads. He inherited from his father a love of learning and a gift for poetry. It was like the plucky, undersized lad to stand up for the principles of his father, twice jailed for the crime of being a dissenter, and to refuse an offer to pay his expenses at the university, since admittance there involved a profession of membership in the Church of England.

DR. ISAAC WATTS

Watts prepared for the ministry deliberately, and became pastor of an Independent meeting in Mark Lane, London. Almost at once his health broke, and the rest of his life was a struggle between duty and weakness. Invited by Sir Thomas Abney, a distinguished dissenter, to spend a week in his magnificent house at Theobalds in Hertfordshire, Watts remained as an honored guest of the family for the rest of his life, some thirty-six years. He gave such service as he could to his long-suffering congregation in London, and managed to write many books, useful in their day, which gave him high reputation in university circles. He was probably the most widely esteemed dissenter of his time; but he himself regarded his " Psalms and Hymns " as incomparably the greatest work he did for the Church.

SOME POINTS FOR DISCUSSION

1. In looking over a line of old Sunday school hymn books, say from 1835 forward, one is struck with the considerable proportion of children's songs dealing with dying and the life after death. These songs reflect the tone of evangelical piety that prevailed among their elders: what the great novelist, George Eliot, described sarcastically as " otherworldliness." It was a time when Dr. Mühlenberg's " I would not live alway " was a favorite for church use.

Then, gradually, the tone of piety began to change. " One world at a time," people began to say, " and now for this world, where our duty lies. It is more pious to rectify a foul drain, to minister to bodily suffering, to show the way to self-help, and to equalize the distribution of the good things of life, than it is to sit and dream of heaven." In our day the reaction from " other-worldliness " is pretty complete. The heaven that lay about us once and then got far enough away to seem like a foreign country, has now to very many lost all reality whatever. How seldom now are these old-time hymns of heaven given out in our churches!

This present situation suggests certain questions. Has the hope of heaven any proper place in Christian experience or in our gospel message to others? Is it right to teach children to sing of heaven; and if not, what is a suitable age at which those who love them might begin to make " mention of her glory " ? Or are there good reasons for thinking the time has arrived for expunging the songs of the heavenly home from our church hymnals?

2. There are, no doubt, different types of hymns of heaven and room for a choice. In one familiar type the singer finds the body vile and the world evil. He turns to the inward vision of a risen body and a dwelling place free from temptations, and passionately longs for the deliverance of death. This type came originally from the monks, " in retreat " from the world, and their rhapsodies are not for everyone. St. Paul would have understood them and loved them, but for most people hymns of this type need watching in the interests of sincerity.

This hymn of Watts is of a very different type. It is less ecstatic. And it breathes no desire to depart. It is the song of a young man who is at work and at play in the open fields of life where God put him, and likes it. He does not want to go home till after sunset. He loves life. He loves the vision of heaven, too, at twilight or when things go wrong, though he does not

cherish the thought of coming to the brink of the narrow sea. But "A Prospect of Heaven makes Death
easy ": so Dr. Watts entitled his verses. He meant that
such a prospect helps to overcome the perfectly natural
shrinking youth feels at the thought of death. And one
sometimes wonders if for many of us, for most perhaps,
this is not the most sincere and helpful song of heaven
ever written.

3. A recent writer in *The Harvard Theological
Review*, commenting on the loveliness of this hymn,
complains that Watts is as confident in regard to
heaven's features and geography as of the country
around Theobald's, and he is tempted to exclaim, " No
such topography for me! " Is that attitude just?

At the farewell dinner in New York to Charles
Dickens, at the end of his last visit to this country, the
brilliant George William Curtis, in closing his speech,
turned to the guest and, bending toward him, said:
" Old ocean bear him safely over! England welcome
him with the blossoms of May! " Is not that the
thought running through the words before us? Not
the topography of heaven, not the landscape of the undiscovered country — only the thought of crossing the
narrow sea to find those things of which spring and
May blossoms are the symbol: green pastures of peace,
the pleasant company of the pure-hearted, the sunlight
of God's Presence over all.

IV

JESUS, LOVER OF MY SOUL

THE TEXT OF THE HYMN

1   Jesus, Lover of my soul,
      Let me to Thy bosom fly,
    While the nearer waters roll,
      While the tempest still is high:
    Hide me, O my Saviour, hide,
      Till the storm of life is past;
    Safe into the haven guide,
      O receive my soul at last.

2   Other refuge have I none;
      Hangs my helpless soul on Thee;
    Leave, ah! leave me not alone,
      Still support and comfort me.
    All my trust on Thee is stayed,
      All my help from Thee I bring;
    Cover my defenceless head
      With the shadow of Thy wing.

3   Wilt Thou not regard my call?
      Wilt Thou not accept my prayer?
    Lo, I sink, I faint, I fall!
      Lo, on Thee I cast my care;
    Reach me out Thy gracious hand!
      While I of Thy strength receive,
    Hoping against hope I stand,
      Dying, and behold I live!

4   Thou, O Christ, art all I want;
    More than all in Thee I find:
    Raise the fallen, cheer the faint,
    Heal the sick, and lead the blind.
    Just and holy is Thy Name;
    I am all unrighteousness;
    False and full of sin I am,
    Thou art full of truth and grace.

5   Plenteous grace with Thee is found,
    Grace to cover all my sin;
    Let the healing streams abound;
    Make and keep me pure within.
    Thou of life the Fountain art,
    Freely let me take of Thee;
    Spring Thou up within my heart,
    Rise to all eternity.

Rev. Charles Wesley, 1740

NOTE. The text is taken from John and Charles Wesley's *Hymns and Sacred Poems* of 1740, with no change except for the printing of the first word in the English rather than the Latin form.

This, perhaps the best loved of all English hymns, is associated with the beginnings of the wonderful Methodist Movement in the eighteenth century, of which John Wesley was the leader and his brother Charles the poet laureate.

THE WESLEYS AND THEIR HYMNS

About the time when Isaac Watts was writing and publishing his sacred songs, two sons were born in the parsonage of the village of Epworth to the Rev. Samuel Wesley and his noble wife Susannah, " Mother of the Wesleys." She was, in fact, the mother of nineteen of them. John was born in 1703, and Charles on Decem-

CHARLES WESLEY

ber 18 of the very year — 1707 — in which Watts published those *Hymns and Spiritual Songs* that changed the worship of the Independent meeting-houses. The two brothers were destined to carry on Watts's work, and to win new triumphs for hymn singing in England. So it is worth while to note that the atmosphere of the parsonage was decidedly contemptuous of the old Psalm singing, as it was then carried on in village churches. As rector of one of them the father had to endure it. But he did not suffer it gladly, and said some very harsh things about it. He was himself a poet, and his sons inherited not only their poetic gifts but their purpose to write something to take the place of what John called the " scandalous doggerel " of the old metrical Psalms.

Y   The two boys grew up together in the Epworth parsonage, were at Oxford University together, were both ordained as clergymen of the Church of England, and in October, 1735, sailed together for the new colony of Georgia. John went as a missionary; Charles nominally, at least, as secretary to General Oglethorpe, Governor of the colony. In John's kit there was a copy of Watts's *Psalms and Hymns*. And he was especially impressed by the constant singing of a group of German Moravian colonists on board. He learned from them what spiritual songs can do for the spiritual life. He studied German so as to translate some of those so dear to his fellow voyagers. In Charleston he published his first collection, and in Savannah was brought before the grand jury, charged with introducing unauthorized hymns into church worship.

Neither brother was successful as a missionary, perhaps because at that time their religion was of a rather severe and formal type. It was the remarkable spiritual experiences they passed through among the Moravians in London, after their return from America, that first gave to both brothers the peace and joy of a confident faith. These experiences changed their lives and determined their future careers. Charles started out as an itinerant preacher. John established the first of those meetings, called " societies," that were the germ of the Methodist Church. He went on translating and writing hymns until organizing and preaching absorbed all his energies.

But in Charles's heart the new happiness seemed to open a fountain of spiritual song that never ceased to flow. He was naturally a poet, and now the writing of religious verse became to him nothing less than a passion. In recording a horseback accident on one of his preaching tours, he notes that his sprains and bruises and stunned head " spoiled my making hymns until next day." Every experience of his own, every scene and occasion of the Methodist revival, became the inspiration of a new hymn. He wrote his first within a day or two of his conversion. He dictated his last to his wife from his deathbed, " in age and feebleness extreme." The whole number is little if at all short of seven thousand. The best of them are perhaps as good as ever were written. Most of them have some touch of hand or flash of thought that suggests a poet rather than a manufacturer.

The unchurched masses among whom the Wesleys worked had of course no preference in favor of Psalms. They quickly caught up the new songs, and the singing became a characteristic feature of the field meetings. As the work went on, the hymns served as an outlet for the extravagant enthusiasm of the converts, and at

the same time kept its expression within limits of reality
and refinement. They were printed in cheap tracts and
booklets for distribution among the people. As "societies" were formed, new hymns were provided for
the class meeting, the children, and the occasions of worship, until finally, in 1780, John Wesley gathered up
four hundred and eighty-six of Charles's compositions,
with some others, into a permanent *Collection of Hymns
for the use of the people called Methodists.*

Charles Wesley was a different type of man from his
great brother: not so commanding a personality, a helper
rather than a leader, a poet with all a poet's moods,
even moods of deep depression, emotional and impetuous,
But probably he was the more lovable of the two men,
with a great gift of winning hearts. The future of the
Methodist Movement lay very heavy on his own heart.
He saw it drifting away from its moorings within the
established Church. He loved his Church with all his
heart and felt no sympathy whatever with his brother's
arrangements for establishing a separate denomination
of Methodists in England and America. He wished
the Methodist societies to remain as a part of the
Church of England. This end he was unable to accom-
plish against his brother's purpose, but as still a clergyman of that Church, he died on March 29, 1788, and
was buried in the yard of his parish church, Marylebone.
"His least praise," his brother said, "was his talent
for poetry."

THE HYMN AND ITS AUTHORSHIP

There are several differing stories of the romantic
origin of "Jesus, Lover of my soul." The most familiar

represents Charles Wesley seated at an open window during a storm, or sometimes on the deck of a vessel laboring under a gale. Then a dove (or sea bird), with its strength all spent, flies to his bosom to find a refuge from the elements. And that inspired the hymn. All these stories cannot be true, and there is no reason to believe that there is a word of truth in any of them. It remains a mystery that worthy people should care to circulate these apocryphal "incidents" of which the popular books are so full.

We do not, in fact, know anything of the occasion of this lyric, except that it is entitled "In Temptation," and sounds like a real cry for help out of such an experience. And there is no absolute assurance that Charles Wesley wrote it. It may have been written by John. The editors of the English *Wesleyan Methodist Hymn Book* of 1875 went so far as to affix simply the letter *W* to this hymn, as a token that they did not know to which of the brothers it should be ascribed.

The matter stands in this way. The brothers printed jointly three volumes of their earlier verses in 1739, 1740, and 1742, with pretty much the same title — *Hymns and Sacred Poems. Published by John Wesley, M.A., and Charles Wesley, M.A.* This one appeared at page 67 of the 1740 volume. There is nothing in this or the other volumes to show which brother wrote any particular poem. Evidently the Wesleys wished it so. In course of time a tradition grew up that only the translations were John's and all the original verse was Charles's. This, we now know, is a mistake, and John's share is much greater than was supposed.

What, then, is to be said of "Jesus, Lover of my soul"? Which brother wrote it?

Anyone familiar with the Wesleyan poems will say that this one is more in the style and manner of those we know to be Charles's than of those we know to be John's. We can go further. John showed later a dislike of anything approaching familiarity in intercourse with God, and especially of the use of terms of human endearment. He turned bitterly against the London Moravians he had loved so well, when they printed hymns with offensive amatory and fleshly images. In a sermon of 1789 he said that familiarity does not so well suit the mouth of a worm of the earth when addressing himself to the God of heaven, and went on, " I have indeed particularly endeavored in all the hymns which are addressed to our blessed Lord, to avoid every fondling expression, and to speak as to the most-high God; to Him that is ' in glory equal with the Father, in majesty co-eternal.' "

Now if John's feeling about such matters was the same in 1740 as in 1789, and there are good reasons for thinking it was, then it is practically certain that he would not have written the lines,

> " Jesu, Lover of my Soul,
> Let me to Thy Bosom fly."

John, as the elder brother, took the privilege of criticizing his brother's poems very freely. There were many expressions in them which he did not like, and he often altered them before printing. That he did not quite approve the expressions in this hymn is shown by the fact that in selecting Charles's contributions to the large permanent hymn book of 1780, he left it out altogether. It was not inserted until after his death. On the whole, it seems that we may ascribe " Jesus,

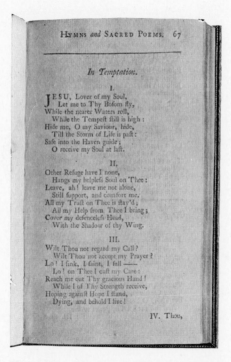

In Temptation.

I.

JESU, Lover of my Soul,
  Let me to Thy Bosom fly,
While the nearer Waters roll,
  While the Tempest still is high :
Hide me, O my Saviour, hide,
  Till the Storm of Life is past :
Safe into the Haven guide ;
  O receive my Soul at last.

II.

Other Refuge have I none,
  Hangs my helpless Soul on Thee :
Leave, ah ! leave me not alone,
  Still support, and comfort me.
All my Trust on Thee is stay'd ;
  All my Help from Thee I bring ;
Cover my defenceless Head,
  With the Shadow of thy Wing.

III.

Wilt Thou not regard my Call ?
  Wilt Thou not accept my Prayer ?
Lo ! I sink, I faint, I fall ——
  Lo ! on Thee I cast my Care :
Reach me out Thy gracious Hand !
  While I of Thy Strength receive,
Hoping against Hope I stand,
  Dying, and behold I live !

IV. Thou,

THE FIRST PRINTING OF THE HYMN

Lover of my soul " to Charles Wesley with a fair degree
of assurance. The only absolute proof would be the
finding of an autograph draft of it in the masses of
Wesleyan manuscripts in the London Conference Office.

SOME POINTS FOR DISCUSSION

1. Many people have claimed John Wesley's privilege
of criticizing this lyric, notably that great lover of
sacred song, the late William E. Gladstone. A friend had
expressed in his hearing a warm admiration for it, and he
had emphatically dissented. And his feelings on the
subject were so strong that he was moved to write out
his objections, even though immediately about to un-
dergo an operation for cataract.

Criticisms of things we love are not very welcome.
But it might be worth while to examine the hymn
anew in the light of Gladstone's objections: (1) That
it has no unity. A number of ideas are jumbled together rather than interwoven. " This is not a whole,
for the parts seem to have no relation to one another."
The theme clearly is that of a soul under stress of a
great temptation calling upon Christ for help. Is that
theme carried through consistently enough to give unity?
(2) That the metaphors are constantly changing and
crossing each other in such a way as to cause confusion.
Thus Christ is at once a Refuge from a storm at sea,
a Pilot into port, an overshadowing Wing, a good
Physician, and finally a Fountain of life. What is to be
said in explanation or defense on this point? (3) That
" it has no procession. Every hymn should surely have
a movement calm, solemn, and continuous. These zig-
zags are out of keeping with the nature of the com-

position. They jar the mind of a reader and set him questioning where he is and where he is going." Is it true that there is no development of thought in the hymn? Or is it just possible that there is really a continuous "procession" of thought in which for some reason Mr. Gladstone's mind has failed to join and has remained stationary?

2. Apart from criticism, the question has often been raised whether a lyric so tender and so deeply felt should be used in public worship or reserved for private devotion. Mr. Ellerton, the hymn writer, confesses that to him " Jesus, Lover of my soul " lies on the very border line between the two. An English bishop thinks it " inexpressibly shocking " to put such words into the mouth of a large and mixed gathering of people. Quaintly enough, actual investigation in the tramps' ward proved this to be one of three hymns most popular with English tramps. The other two are " Lead, kindly Light " and " Abide with me."

3. John Wesley was surely right in objecting to familiarity and fondling expressions in our hymns. Might it not be well if some of our modern gospel songs were submitted to that test? It is, however, a question how far these objections apply to the first two lines of this hymn. Charles Wesley used " Lover " in the divine and not our human sense, taking it from the apocryphal book, *The Wisdom of Solomon:* " But thou sparest all, because they are Thine, O Lord, Thou Lover of souls." The imagery of the second line is that of St. John lying on the bosom of his Lord. It is true, however, that we are not all St. Johns. A host of editors have proposed alterations of these lines, and have succeeded in completely spoiling the poetry of them.

4. The editors have also tried their hand on the third line. Some of us remember when "While the billows near me roll" was the familiar reading. Is there any occasion for alteration? Dr. Julian says: "In life, as in nature, storms are local. One ship may be dashed hither and thither by the fury of the nearer waters, whilst another is sleeping in the far distance on a throbless sea. Men cry for help, not against dangers which are both distant and undefined, but out of the depths of their immediate troubles."

5. *The Hymnal revised* is one of the very few books that print the whole of these five verses just as "W" wrote them. The custom is to omit the third verse. But then the third verse is exceptionally good. And if we wish a four-verse hymn, is it not worth while to consider the dropping out of the fourth verse and the retaining of this?

V

CHILDREN OF THE HEAVENLY KING

THE TEXT OF THE HYMN

1 Children of the heavenly King,
   As ye journey, sweetly sing;
   Sing your Saviour's worthy praise,
   Glorious in His works and ways.

2 We are traveling home to God
   In the way the fathers trod;
   They are happy now, and we
   Soon their happiness shall see.

3 Shout, ye little flock and blest;
   You on Jesus' throne shall rest;
   There your seat is now prepared,
   There your kingdom and reward.

4 Lift your eyes, ye sons of light,
   Zion's city is in sight;
   There our endless home shall be,
   There our Lord we soon shall see.

5 Fear not, brethren; joyful stand
   On the borders of your land;
   Jesus Christ, your Father's Son,
   Bids you undismayed go on.

6 Lord, obediently we go,
   Gladly leaving all below;
   Only Thou our Leader be,
   And we still will follow Thee.

Rev. John Cennick, 1742

NOTE: The text here given is abridged (to its great gain) from the twelve verses of the original as printed by Cennick, in the third part of his *Sacred Hymns for the Children of God, in the days of their pilgrimage,* London, 1742. The verses selected are the original first, second, fifth, sixth, seventh, and eighth, printed without change, except of spelling and punctuation.

This is one of the earlier hymns of the great eighteenth century revival, written by an eager young convert, John Cennick. He became a Methodist lay preacher first of all, but soon ranged himself with Whitefield as opposed to Wesley's theology. In the end he found his true home among the most simple-hearted of all God's people, the Moravians.

CENNICK'S STRANGE EXPERIENCE

When Cennick printed his first little book of hymns he prefixed a sort of confession or spiritual auto-biography. It began, *"Perhaps it may not be unuseful for some of those, who may read the following Verses, to know the Manner wherein* GOD *has dealt with the Soul of him who wrote them."* That is still good advice to us if we wish to study Cennick's, or indeed any of the hymns of the great Revival. Those eighteenth-century hymns are different from most later hymns. They are the outpourings of converts who have passed through such struggles in finding peace that ever after-wards spiritual experiences seemed to them the most real thing in life, and the inward state of one's soul the only thing that mattered much. The common feature of these experiences, but the feature hardest for an easy-going twentieth century Christian to understand, is the dark despairs and acute agonies they had to endure under the grip of "the conviction of sin." Some of them were reduced to a disorder of mind and body close to the borders of insanity; but one and all of these converts credited not only their deliverance but their sufferings also to the hand of God. Cennick's case was peculiar only in the degree of his sufferings and in his ability to express the joy of his deliverance.

He was born in the English town of Reading on December 12, 1718, being eleven years younger than Charles Wesley. His family was respectable but somewhat impoverished. His mother trained him carefully in the ways of Church of England religion, and the child appears to have been unusually assiduous in attending St. Laurence's Church. What he and many like him seem to have gained from the religious training of the time was a conscience made sensitive by the fear of penalties, and a constant dread of God that spoiled one's pleasures but was not allayed by observing church ordinances.

When Cennick went up to London to learn a trade he fell, no doubt, into more careless ways of living; until, while walking in Cheapside one day in 1735, he was suddenly stricken down with an overwhelming sense of sin, as though felled by God's hand. He sank at once into an abject fear and hopeless despondency, from which through two bitter years he found no escape.

Within his conscience seared like a hot iron; without "everything seemed strange and wild," and there was no refuge in heaven or earth. He longed to hide himself in some lonely cave and to sustain life on acorns and leaves; hoping indeed that he might not sustain it and yet afraid of the death he craved. He tried fasting, and in his weakened condition began to see apparitions and to hear approaching footfalls of the Devil. He shrank from the faces of men, and thought men shrank from him and that friends grew cold.

Finally—it was in August, 1737—he resolved in his

J. Cennick.

despair to cast himself on God's mercy and leave the rest with Him. Still waiting on Him in dejection, at home one day in September, he heard "the Saint's Bell

ring at St. Laurence's Church for Prayers." He felt
constrained to attend. *"Near the end of the Psalms,
when these Words were read:* Great are the Troubles
of the Righteous but the LORD delivereth him out of
them all! And he that putteth his Trust in GOD shall
not be destitute: *I had just Room to think,* Who can
be more destitute than me? *when I was overwhelmed
with Joy, I believed there was Mercy. My Heart
danced for Joy, and my dying Soul reviv'd! I heard
the Voice of JESUS saying,* I am thy Salvation. *I no
more groaned under the Weight of Sin. The Fear of
Hell was taken away, and being sensible that CHRIST
loved me, and died for me, I rejoiced in GOD, my*
SAVIOUR."

So sudden a change brings its own perplexities.
Cennick found help in Whitefield's newly printed
Journal, and sought the counsel of both him and John
Wesley. They encouraged him and found a position
for him as a teacher in a school for coal miners' children
at Kingswood. There he at once began to preach to
the miners and attained what, historically speaking, is
his special distinction: he was in all probability the
first of the " lay preachers " of Methodism.

"HYMNS FOR THE CHILDREN OF GOD"

George Whitefield, and not Wesley, had been the
original field preacher, and in the early days of the
revival the two men had worked hand in hand. But
in 1739, after Whitefield had gone to America on his
revival tour, the Wesleys put out a pamphlet bitterly
attacking the Calvinistic doctrine of Predestination.
" My dear Brothers," Whitefield wrote, " why did you

throw out the bone of contention? " It was a bone of contention indeed. Soon afterward John Wesley notes a marked change in Cennick's manner toward him.

When Whitefield came home from America in 1741, the rift widened into a permanent breach between the Methodists and Calvinists, with Whitefield as the leader of the Calvinists. Cennick broke with the Wesleys, became a helper in Whitefield's revival work, and so continued for four years.

He had begun to write hymns while a Methodist, but it was during those four years that he printed all of his hymns which are now remembered. In emulation of the Wesleys on the Methodist side, it may have been; but whether so or not, he was for those years as industrious a maker of hymns as was Charles Wesley himself, printing very nearly five hundred.

Cennick began to print his hymns in 1741 as *Sacred Hymns for the Children of God, in the days of their pilgrimage*. So rapid was his production that a second and a third part appeared in 1742. In the year following he published in two parts *Sacred Hymns for the use of Religious Societies. Generally composed in* DIA-LOGUES. By societies he meant companies of people who met together, apart from the church services, to cultivate the religious life. By " dialogues " he meant what we call singing antiphonally or responsively. He had in mind the Moravian custom of arranging the people in separate choirs, according to age or sex: one choir singing the first line or lines of each verse, the other responding with the line or lines following. And in his little book he made this practicable by printing some lines of the verses in roman type, and some in italics; like this:

> "We sing to Thee, Thou Son of GOD!
>   Who Sav'd us by thy Grace:
>   *We praise Thee, Son of Man! whose Blood*
>   *Redeem'd our fallen Race."*

The Moravians already had formed societies in London, and very evidently Cennick was being attracted toward them, just as John Wesley was; but in Cennick's case it was the call of the blood inherited from a Moravian ancestry and still at work through the quaint compellings of heredity. Cennick did not resist the call. He left Whitefield and joined the Moravians. His later years were spent partly in the spread of Moravianism in England and Ireland, and partly in visiting Germany. He came back to London in great feebleness in June of 1755, and on the fourth of July died there.

He was a man "rather below the middle stature," Rev. Matthew Wilks says, "of a fair countenance, but of a fairer mind. A good understanding, an open temper, and a tender heart characterized the man." He was distinguished by "unaffected humility, deadness to the world, a life of communion with God, and a cheerful reliance on a crucified Saviour." All of which is a good hearing. If John Wesley dubbed Cennick "that weak man," we can understand it. A follower who vacillates is always weak to a great and single-hearted leader.

THE STORY OF THE HYMN

Of Cennick's familiar hymns, the one we are now studying appeared in 1742 in the third part of the *Sacred Hymns for the Children of God.* "We sing to Thee, Thou Son of God" appeared a year later in *Hymns*

for the use of Religious Societies. Whitefield liked
Cennick's hymns, and liked his idea of singing in
"Dialogue." It was because Whitefield put these two
and others of Cennick's hymns into the hymn book
he made for his London Tabernacle in 1753 that they
became so widely known and sung.

Cennick was very modest about his hymns. "*Of
either good poetry, or fine language therein, indeed there
is none. A Child wrote them, who is but a young Student in* CHRIST'S *school.*" But they were intended to
be songs and not tracts in verse. Cennick was a great
believer in "the ministry of song."

It would not be possible to connect our present hymn,
or any other of Cennick's hymns, with any particular
outward event or special experience of his life. Nevertheless we cannot catch the spiritual beauty of this
hymn of courage and good cheer until we connect it with
the life Cennick was leading. Truly these itinerant
preachers of Wesley and Whitefield had a hard time of it
— in journeyings often, in weariness and painfulness, in
hunger and thirst, and, most of all, in perils from their
own countrymen. Their own countrymen, even the best
of them, thought them disturbers of the settled order,
and the ruder, illiterate element of the people seems
to have hated them and their gospel instinctively.
Wherever these preachers went, they were met and surrounded by a rough and often brutal hostility, sometimes egged on by the local authorities, including even
the clergy.

In June, 1741, Cennick went with some friends to
preach at Swindon. But before he could begin, he
writes, the mob " fired guns over our heads, holding
the muzzles so near our faces, that Howell Harris and

myself were both made as black as tinkers with the powder. We were not affrighted, but opened our breasts, telling them we were ready to lay down our lives for our doctrine. Then they got dust out of the highway, and covered us all over; and then played an engine upon us, which they filled out of the stinking ditches. While they played upon brother Harris, I preached; and, when they turned the engine upon me, he preached. This continued till they spoiled the engine; and then they threw whole buckets of water and mud over us. Mr. Goddard, a leading gentleman of the town, lent the mob his guns, halberd, and engine, and bade them use us as badly as they could, only not to kill us; and he himself sat on horseback the whole time, laughing to see us thus treated."

It is such experiences as these, of the very time when our hymn was written, that make its actual setting. And out of them it shines in all of its spiritual beauty — the pluck of an unconquerable purpose, the serenity of an untroubled faith, the good cheer of an incorruptible hope.

SOME POINTS FOR DISCUSSION

1. The literary critics are not always very kind to our hymns. But we must not hit back and say that the critics themselves are not so spiritual-minded as they ought to be. Sometimes they may be right. As Mr. Toplady said, in the preface to his hymn book in 1776: " God is the God of *Truth, of Holiness, and of Elegance.* Whoever, therefore, has the honor to compose, or to compile, anything that may constitute a part of His worship, should keep those three particulars, constantly, in view." It may be that some of our hymns are not worthy of the God of *Elegance.*

It is, then, comforting to know that Mr. Palgrave, Professor of Poetry at Oxford, and editor of *The Golden Treasury* — still generally regarded as the standard of our lyrical poetry — did not hesitate to include these six verses of Cennick's in his later *Treasury of Sacred Song*. These six, it may be added, are only the half of the original hymn. But they are the better half.

2. These studies are not intended to be "preachy." (The writer once read a sermon on this hymn preached by Canon Duncan at St. Stephen's, Newcastle-upon-Tyne; and he still likes the hymn.) But with his readers' consent he would venture to say that in his opinion the injunction in the second line of this hymn is as good advice as we are likely to get in this world. The road to heaven is not so hard for most of us as Cennick found it; but it is never easy going. And he who can meet the hard places with a song is the best traveler.

And that is the great argument in favor of committing hymns to memory. You cannot always carry *The Hymnal* in your grip "as ye journey."

3. May not Cennick's hymn be ranged with Watts's "There is a land of pure delight," as one of the undoubtedly wholesome hymns dealing with the hope of heaven? It is, at all events, one of the few hymns on that subject which young people generally have liked to sing. Of course the buoyant melody, arranged from a movement in an instrumental quartet by Ignaz Joseph Pleyel, helps to keep the hymn alive. Pleyel was an Austrian, and it is odd that the tune was for a century called "German Hymn" by most people.

Cennick's hymn may also be compared with Williams' "Guide me, O Thou Great Jehovah," as being a different treatment of the journey of the Children of Israel to the promised country. Williams' hymn is a prayer for help from the dangers and difficulties of the road. Cennick pictures a sunny-hearted pilgrim, who thinks nothing of the perils of the road in view of the glory beyond that shines on them. But Watts, to get back to " There is a land of pure delight," leaves the Children of Israel appraising the width of Jordan from its bank where they are gathered, while he climbs the hill with Moses to " view the landscape o'er."

VI

CHRISTIANS, AWAKE! SALUTE THE HAPPY MORN

THE TEXT OF THE HYMN

1   Christians, awake! salute the happy morn,
Whereon the Saviour of the world was born;
Rise to adore the mystery of love,
Which hosts of angels chanted from above;
With them the joyful tidings first begun
Of God Incarnate and the Virgin's Son.

2   Then to the watchful shepherds it was told,
Who heard the angelic herald's voice: " Behold,
I bring good tidings of a Saviour's birth
To you and all the nations upon earth:
This day hath God fulfilled His promised word;
This day is born a Saviour, Christ the Lord."

3   He spake: and straightway the celestial choir
In hymns of joy, unknown before, conspire;
The praises of redeeming love they sang,
And heaven's whole orb with alleluias rang:
God's highest glory was their anthem still,
Peace upon earth, and mutual good will.

4   O may we keep and ponder in our mind
God's wondrous love in saving lost mankind;
Trace we the Babe, who has retrieved our loss,
From His poor manger to His bitter cross;
Treading His steps, assisted by His grace,
Till man's first heavenly state again takes place.

5   Then may we hope, the angelic thrones among,
To sing, redeemed, a glad triumphal song;
He that was born upon this joyful day
Around us all His glory shall display;
Saved by His love, incessant we shall sing
Eternal praise to heaven's Almighty King.

> Arranged from a Christmas poem of John Byrom, 1750: verse 4, line 1; verse 5, line 6, altered

Two of our familiar Christmas hymns are associated with the Methodist side of the eighteenth century revival and with the Wesleys themselves. One of the friends whose help they asked in preparing their first hymn book after they had returned from Georgia was Dr. John Byrom; and he is the author of " Christians, awake! " The other Christmas hymn, " Hark! the herald angels sing," was printed by the Wesleys themselves, in 1739, in the earliest of the three collections they named *Hymns and Sacred Poems.*

JOHN BYROM AND HIS POEMS

There is no need of a lingering look at Dr. Byrom's portrait to assure us that he was what is called a character. From under the low slouched hat with its rim projecting like the prow of a racing yacht, the bewigged head bends forward in an inquisitive intentness; and the face is as striking as the hat, with a ruminating look in the eye and a very whimsical but not unkindly mouth. One notes the crook-handled cane and wonders what the color of the long coat may have been. It must have been a very long coat, for Byrom was conspicuously tall. He speaks in his diary of taking walks with John Wesley. Now Wesley was rather short and slight, dressed in conventional clerical clothes, and a model of neatness, so that the couple walking side by side must have presented something of a spectacle.

Underneath these oddities Byrom was very much a gentleman and something of a scholar, a devoted husband and affectionate father, a loyal friend in fair weather and foul; and in spite of a gift of bubbling humor, he walked the earth in a sort of reverential awe that made life very sacred and God very near.

He was the son of a linen merchant of Manchester, England, near which city he was born in February, 1692; and was thus eighteen years younger than Isaac Watts and eleven years older than John Wesley. The biographical dictionaries sum him up as " poet and stenographer," and he was already both of these while still at college in Cambridge. While there he invented a new system of shorthand, and also printed in *The Spectator* for October 6, 1714, a playful pastoral poem called " Colin and Phœbe," which attracted more attention and admiration than anything he wrote afterwards. When through college he went to the continent to study medicine, and though he never won his diploma he was called " Doctor " for the rest of his life.

Byrom returned to England in 1718 and married a cousin. His elder brother had inherited the family property, and he started to earn a living by teaching his shorthand. His pupils paid him five guineas and swore an oath to keep the secret of his system. They liked him and no doubt had their fun out of him, calling him " the Grand Master "; and among them were some very distinguished men.

Between Byrom and the Wesleys were two bonds — a common love of shorthand and of religion. Charles

Drawn by G. Clint A.R.A.   Engraved by A. Duncan.

JOHN BYROM M.A.

From an original Drawing in the possession of the Publisher

DR. JOHN BYROM

Wesley adopted Byrom's system at a very early date, and soon persuaded John to adopt it. Many of their hymns, the diary of Charles, and the vast and invaluable " Journal " of John Wesley, were all written in Byrom's shorthand.

There was not only a warm friendship between the men, but a religious sympathy deeper than the differences of their temperaments and theological views. Byrom was known at Manchester as a High Churchman and a Jacobite — an adherent of the Pretender as against the king. But he did not allow his churchmanship to interfere with his wide religious sympathies. It is indeed probable that his deep spirituality alienated him from the average clergy of that day and prevented him from becoming a clergyman himself. He was at heart a mystic, caring more about real personal relations with God than about systems of theology or church organizations. He never became a Methodist, and probably never had the peculiar type of religious experience that the great revival produced. But he was sympathetic with the religious work of the Wesleys, attended their services frequently, and was their warm friend in days when so many despised and ridiculed them.

The Wesleys consulted him about their first collection of hymns of 1738 and asked him to contribute some. He responded with excellent advice and with translations of two French mystical hymns. One of these seems to have been the " Come, Saviour Jesus! from above," that became a well-known Methodist hymn and is in use up to the present day. It may be that John Wesley's hand touched it up here and there, as was his way. It is not likely that Byrom helped the Wesleys in actual religious activities. Meditation and study and debate were more to his taste than activity. He liked to do his own thinking and to cultivate lettered ease; to let the world wag while he contemplated it with what he calls in one of his poems "calm content."

In 1740 Byrom's brother died and he inherited the family property. Henceforward shorthand was rather a hobby than a means of livelihood, and he had all the more time for writing poetry. He had always had a gift for meter and for rhyming, and it got so that he seemed to think in verse, as Mr. Henley puts it. Every subject he wanted to argue about or poke fun at seemed to him a suitable subject for poetry. Descriptions, narratives, criticisms, speeches, essays, theological disquisitions as well as hymns — they were all in verse. It is fair, however, to remember that he wrote for the amusement of himself and friends and seldom printed his verses. They were not collected and published until after his death. His versifying, as he grew older, became more and more religious in its character, and it came to an end only with a long illness. He died on September 26, 1763, and his poems were published in two volumes at Manchester in 1773.

On July 12 of that year John Wesley read them on a journey from Liverpool to Birmingham, and was delighted with them. He said they showed all the wit of Dean Swift, with more learning and piety, and expressed some of the finest sentiments that ever appeared in English arrayed in the strongest colors of poetry. The present writer owns a copy of the same edition of the poems that Mr. Wesley read, but has not found there all that he did. The wit and learning and piety are all there, and the charm of a quaint personality, but the

" colors of poetry " have faded out somewhat. Byrom's verse will have few readers nowadays, but he will be remembered by one of the wittiest of epigrams:

> " God bless the King, I mean the Faith's Defender;
>   God bless — no Harm in blessing — the Pretender;
>   But who Pretender is, or who is King,
>   God bless us all — that's quite another Thing."

He will be remembered also by this Christmas carol that may very likely be sung as long as the celebration of that day survives among English-speaking people.

" CHRISTMAS DAY FOR DOLLY "

On the walls of the librarian's room of the Chetham Library at Manchester hangs the neatly framed original manuscript of Byrom's Christmas poem, on a very crowded sheet of note paper. It bears the title " Christmas Day for Dolly." And from this poem, by omitting some of the lines and arranging the remainder into verses which can be sung, our Christmas hymn, " Christians, awake! " has been made.

Francis Arthur Jones, in his *Famous Hymns and their Authors,* tells an attractive little story about the poem. " It was written in 1745, and the story of its composition is a pretty tale. John Byrom, the author, had several children, but, like many another father, he had his favorite. This child was a little girl named Dolly, who afterwards became Mrs. * Dorothy Byrom. A few days prior to Christmas, 1745, Mr. Byrom, after having had a romp with the favored Dolly, promised to write her something for Christmas Day. It was to

* Used, at that period, as a courtesy title.

Christmas Day for Dolly

...ians awake, salute the happy Morn
...reon the Saviour of the World was born
... to adore the Mystery of Love
...ch Hosts of Angels chanted from above
...th them the joyfull Tidings first begun
...n to the watchfull Shepherds it was told
... heard th' Angelic Herald's Voice—behold
...ou...
...ring. ... Tidings of the Saviour's Birth
...und all the Nations upon Earth
...hath God fulfill'd the promised Word
...is day is born y.e Saviour X.t the Lord
... David city ... ye shall find
... long fortold redeemer of Mankind
...rapt up in swadling cloaths, be this the sign
... Cratch contains the holy Babe divine
...te spake, & straightway the celestial Quire
...Hymns of Joy unknown, before conspire
... Praises of redeeming Love, they sung
...d Heav'n whole Orb w.th Hallelujahs rung
...od Highest Glory was their ...
...eace upon Earth & mutual good Will

To Bethlehem straight th' enlightned Shepherds ran
To see the Wonder God had wrought for man
They saw their Saviour as the Angel said
The swadled Infant in the Manger laid
Joseph & Mary a distressed Pair
Guard the sole Object of th' almighty's Care
To human Eyes none present but they two
Where Heav'n was pouring it concentred View
Amaz'd the wondrous Story they proclaim
The ... ...
The first apostles of his Infant Fame
But Mary kept & ponder'd in her Heart
The heav'nly Vision w.th the Swains impart
They to their flocks & praising God return
With Hearts no doubt y.t did within them burn

Let us like these good Shepherds then employ
Our gratefull Voices to proclaim the Joy
Like Mary let us ponder in our Mind
Gods wondrous Love in saving lost Mankind
Artless & watchfull as these favour'd Swains
While Virgin Meekness in the Heart remains
Trace we the Babe who has retriev'd our loss
From his poor Manger to his bitter Cross
Follow we him who has our Cause maintain'd
And Man's first heav'nly State shall be regain'd

THE POEM AS BYROM WROTE IT

be written specially for herself, and no one else. The child, highly honored and delighted, did not fail to remind her father of his promise each day as Christmas drew nearer. On the morning of the great day, when she ran down to breakfast, she found several presents waiting for her. Among these was an envelope addressed to her in her father's handwriting. It was the first thing she opened, and to her great delight, proved to be a Christmas carol addressed to her, and to her alone." Mr. Jones goes on to add that the present creased and crumpled state of the original manuscript comes " probably from being carried about in Miss Dolly's pocket."

It makes a pretty story and one would like to believe it. But how can we? The title of the manuscript does show that Byrom gave it to his daughter. But that he wrote it for her especially is less evident, because the words " for Dolly " are added in pencil, as though they were an afterthought. And there is no evidence whatever that Byrom wrote the poem during Dolly's childhood. She was born on April 26, 1730, and the earliest date we have for the hymn is Christmas, 1750, at which time Dolly was quite a grown-up young lady. In nearby Manchester there was a young man, John Wainwright, who had some part in the music of the old Church of St. Mary the Virgin, now the Cathedral. He, too, had a copy of Byrom's poem and saw its possibilities as a Christmas carol. He divided it into verses and composed for it the delightful tune to which it is still sung. And on " Xmas, 1750, the singing men and boys, with Mr. Wainwright " (in other words, the choir of St. Mary's) paid Dr. Byrom — or was it Dolly? — the compliment of coming out to his home and singing " Christians, awake! " beneath his windows. This in its way is as pleasing an incident as Mr. Jones's little story, and it has the quite inestimable advantage of being true.

The Wesleys did not put their friend's Christmas hymn into any of their hymn books, and it was probably unknown to Toplady and the others who soon began to make Church of England hymn books. But in those days of carol singing Wainwright's tune attracted attention. " It is instinct with the healthy frost and good cheer of the old-fashioned English Christmas"; and it was as a Christmas carol rather than a church hymn that the words and tune so happily mated began their career, and became popular in northern England. The Rev. Caleb Ashworth, a Lancashire man, heard and liked the tune, and put it into his tune book printed in 1760, but he divorced it from Byrom's words and made it a setting for Dr. Watts's version of the Fiftieth Psalm:

> " The God of Glory sends his Summons forth,
>   Calls the *South* Nations, and awakes the *North*."

Ashworth's book had only a local circulation. But in 1784 the Rev. Ralph Harrison, another Lancashire man, included the tune in his tune book. His book became very popular and made the tune widely known. Harrison's book found its way into this country, and in various American editions of " Watts's Psalms " in the first half of the nineteenth century the Fiftieth Psalm is marked to be sung to " Walworth "; and on turning to the tune books we find that Walworth was simply Wainwright's tune under another name. It is unlikely that it was much sung. Congregations of the time were not musical and would shrink from six lines of ten syllables. Perhaps sometimes the choirs attempted to render it for them.

Over in England Byrom's hymn had never been lost sight of. Every Christmas it was sung to Wainwright's tune, but as an out-of-doors carol rather than in church. It was the poet Montgomery who made a church hymn out of it. He arranged it for the hymn book he compiled for his friend, the Rev. Thomas Cotterill, in 1819; and from that book it has passed into most of the important church hymnals both in England and America. The Presbyterians in Scotland and the Methodists in America are exceptional, in that they have not yet learned the pleasure of saluting the happy morn with " Christians, awake! "

SOME POINTS FOR DISCUSSION

1. What is the difference between a Christmas hymn and a Christmas carol? A hymnologist would say that " Hark! the herald angels sing " was a hymn, and that " Christians, awake! " and " O little town of Bethlehem " were carols. Is it because a carol treats the subject with a child's simplemindedness and from a child's point of view? Or does the distinction refer only to the character of the music used?

2. The reader has before him the full text of Byrom's poem as first written, except the last six lines, which he can supply from *The Hymnal revised.* He is in the same position as the editor of a hymn book who wants to use the poem, but is confronted with the problem of arranging it so that it can be sung. Probably no editor ever solved that problem to his complete satisfaction, and the reader can if he pleases apply his own

wits to it and try for a better arrangement. The conditions are:

(1) Some lines must be omitted. The poem is too long for a hymn.

(2) There should be the fewest possible alterations.

(3) The verses must be of six lines to fit Wainwright's tune. Nobody wants to sing it to anything else.

(4) Montgomery made six verses, which are too many. An arrangement in four that kept the train of thought unbroken would be ideal.

3. There are two types of hymn tunes. There are choir tunes, of delicate beauty, that one likes to listen to rather than to sing. And there are people's tunes that make one feel like joining in to swell the volume of sound. " Stockport " is just such a tune. It represents a period when people were getting tired of the old Psalm tunes sung in church, and church musicians were seeking a somewhat lighter and more cheerful type of tune. When one catches the spirit of its bluff heartiness and the swing of its melody it is still quite irresistible. If not sung in our churches as often as one might wish, that may be because it makes no special appeal to the choir, or because our congregations have not become familiar with it.

VII

GUIDE ME, O THOU GREAT JEHOVAH

THE TEXT OF THE HYMN

1   Guide me, O Thou Great Jehovah,
     Pilgrim through this barren land;
  I am weak, but Thou art mighty,
     Hold me with Thy powerful hand:
       Bread of heaven,
     Feed me till I want no more.

2   Open now the crystal fountain,
     Whence the healing stream doth flow;
  Let the fire and cloudy pillar
     Lead me all my journey through:
       Strong Deliverer,
     Be Thou still my Strength and Shield.

3   When I tread the verge of Jordan,
     Bid my anxious fears subside;
  Death of deaths and hell's Destruction,
     Land me safe on Canaan's side:
       Songs of praises
     I will ever give to Thee.

> Written in Welsh by the Rev. William Williams, 1745
> In making an English version, about 1772, he used a
> translation of the first verse already (1771) made by the
> Rev. Peter Williams, and himself translated the second
> and third verses.

NOTE: The text of the three verses as here given is that of the leaflet of 1772 prepared for Lady Huntingdon's College at Trevecca, without change except the capitalizing of " Destruction " in verse three. A fourth verse given there is omitted but is quoted in the course of this chapter.

68

This hymn takes us back to the great revival in the old country and the stirring scenes of the seventeen-forties amid which it was written. But it carries us for the moment across the border into Wales, for it was written originally in the Welsh and not the English language.

THE STORY OF THE HYMN

In our study of " Children of the heavenly King " we left Cennick and Howell Harris at Swindon in 1741, preaching antiphonally. As the mob squirted mud on each in turn, the other preached. Harris was a young Welsh layman of the robust and hearty type; he had already lighted the flame of revival in Wales, while the Wesleys were still in Georgia. He began first to visit from house to house, and then to preach to the people who thronged to hear him. He made many converts and gathered them into " societies "; and he drew to his side many preachers, some of them from the established Church itself. Among them, and the one who most interests us, was William Williams, author of " Guide me, O Thou Great Jehovah."

When John Wesley went on a preaching tour in Wales, he found this band of preachers already at work; and with a great advantage over himself, who could speak no Welsh. Howell Harris was a Calvinist, but he and Wesley loved each other instinctively, and each rejoiced in the other's success. But when the split in the revival forces came in 1741, the Welsh preachers took Whitefield's side. " The people are wounded by scores, and flock under the Word by thousands," Harris wrote him in 1742. And in the year following the Welsh

Calvinistic Methodist Church was organized, with Whitefield in the moderator's chair.

The revival preachers were much hindered by the lack of spiritual and warm-hearted hymns in Welsh to stir the people's hearts. In Wales, as in England, the parish churches were still singing metrical Psalm versions, and spiritual songs were few. Soon after organizing the Calvinistic Methodists, Harris summoned a

THE REV. WILLIAM WILLIAMS

group of preachers to a contest, of a sort not unfamiliar in fervid and musical Wales, at competitive hymn writing. The prize fell easily to William Williams, who had the poet's passion and a gift of verse-writing. Therefore it was not very long before he was recognized as poet laureate of the Welsh revival.

His hymns, with their passion and sweetness, and an underlying tone of pathos, seemed at once to fly abroad as if the winds carried them. He began to gather and print them, under the title of *Halleluiah* in 1744; and in a second part published in 1745 appeared the Welsh original of " Guide me, O Thou Great Jehovah." A new series entitled *Hosannah,* began to appear in 1751, and was complete in 1754. Other volumes followed at later dates. Williams also wrote and published English hymns: fifty-one of them as *Hosannah to the Son of David* in 1759, and seventy-one more as *Gloria in excelsis* in 1772.

" Guide me, O Thou Great Jehovah " had been put into English by another Williams (the Rev. Peter) in 1771. William Williams adopted his colleague's first verse, himself translated the second and third, added a fourth, and printed the whole English version in a leaflet, about 1772, with this heading:

A FAVOURITE HYMN,

sung by

Lady Huntingdon's Young Collegians.

Printed by the desire of many Christian friends.

Lord, give it Thy blessing!

Lady Huntingdon, of whom we shall hear again, was a great lady, whose whole heart and soul were in Whitefield's work. She had founded a college at Trevecca in South Wales to educate young preachers, and it was in the college chapel that the " many Christian friends " had heard the hymn. It plainly made a great impression. Lady Huntingdon put it into the books used in the chapels she had built. Whitefield added it in 1774 to his popular hymn book used in the London Tabernacle. Toplady put it into his collection of 1776, dedicated to the God of Elegance. From these books its use spread far and wide. Few English hymns have started so auspiciously and held the pace so long.

THE POET OF THE WELSH REVIVAL

William Williams was born at Cefn-y-Coed in 1717, of parents who were active dissenters from the Church of England system, which was established by law in Wales also. His education was carried on with a view to making him a physician; but Providence had other uses for him.

On a Sunday morning in 1738 he happened to attend a lifeless service in the parish church of the little village of Talgarth. On leaving the church the congregation, instead of scattering to their homes, gathered about the short, sturdy figure of a man who began to preach from one of the flat gravestones, exhorting the people to repent and escape the wrath to come. The preacher was Howell Harris, and his impassioned oratory could sway such a Welsh crowd as the wind sways the wheat. He reached the heart of young Williams, and changed his life. The young man left the churchyard with the purpose of devoting his life to the ministry.

In 1740, Williams was ordained deacon in the Church of England, and was given a small curacy up in the mountains. But Howell Harris was his real bishop; his heart was with the revival movement and not with the Establishment. With several other clergy of the established Church, he gave up his curacy and joined the dissenting revivalists, though still " in deacon's orders."

He became an itinerant preacher, and never obtained

fuller orders in the ministry of the Church of England.
That his bishop refused them is often stated, but does
not seem to be clearly proved. Whatever the bishop
may have thought of his course, Williams made an
extraordinary record as an itinerant evangelist. He
took the whole of Wales for his parish. His travels for
forty-three years are said to make an average of 2230
miles a year, at a time when there were no railroads and
few stage-coaches. In this way the greater part of
Williams' life was spent, not in a preacher's study, but
in the great world of out of doors. The breaking of
dawn, the play of sunlight and shadow, the changing
cloud effects, the gathering storm, the approach of twilight, and the darkness of night — these were the things
he lived with. The wonderful scenery of his native land,
with its visions of mountain and valley, brooks rushing
down the hills and placid rivers among the fields, the
seashore with its rocks and harbors — all these he saw
every day with a poet's eye.

And just as the gospel story itself seems always to
have the landscape of Palestine for a setting and so
many of Christ's sayings reveal his observation of nature, so Williams' poetry is set in the landscape of
Wales, and his hymns, the Welsh ones especially, are
full of allusions to the scenery amid which he lived.
The world of nature became to him a parable of the
world of grace. Even the unattractive opening of his
" O'er the gloomy hills of darkness " is said to reproduce
an early morning vision of the Prescelly hills looming
dark through the mist, while in the east the dawn was
breaking up the gloom with the promise of a new day.

It was a picturesque life, but it was not an easy one;
for nature is not always kind. It involved much ex-

posure and constant fatigue. It incurred also that menace of the mob of which all these revival preachers were victims. There is still extant a letter of Howell Harris to Whitefield describing an attack of ruffians armed with guns and staves, made upon Williams while preaching in Cardiganshire, in which he was beaten without mercy. And Harris writes that the attack was instigated by " a gentleman of the neighborhood." Such self-sacrificing years of evangelism and those weary thousands of miles sum up the remainder of Williams' life: not that many of the rich or great of the earth were concerned to compute the sum. But his verse must have made him a certain reputation outside of Wales, for the eminently genteel *Gentleman's Magazine* of 1791 gave him quite a nice obituary notice.

" After languishing some time, he finished his course and life together, January 11th, 1791, aged 74." That sounds as if the last long mile had been the hardest of all. He was buried in the churchyard of an obscure Welsh village, and, as the inscription upon his gravestone reads, " He waits here the coming of the Morning Star."

Williams was evidently one of those sweet and wistful souls who cross this world as pilgrims and strangers, with their eyes fixed on a better one. He endured and magnified the rough lot of a revival preacher of those days, abounded in labors, and suffered perils for his Master's sake. His load was lightened a bit by a native sense of humor, but he needed for himself and he preached to others the consolations of the gospel. And it is altogether pleasant to remember him as we sing his pilgrim hymn.

But we should be doing a great injustice to Williams'

memory if we were to think of him simply as the author
of one English hymn that perhaps we like to sing. His
great work as a religious poet was done in his own
Welsh tongue. We who, like John Wesley, cannot speak
Welsh and who know much less of Wales than he did,
can hardly understand how great a place the hymns of
Williams hold in Welsh religious history and Welsh
hearts. On this subject it is better to let one of his
countrymen speak out of his personal knowledge. The
Rev. H. Elvet Lewis, himself a poet, writes: " What Paul
Gerhardt has been to Germany, what Watts has been to
England, that and more has William Williams been to
the little principality of Wales. His hymns have both
stirred and soothed a whole nation for a hundred years;
they have helped to fashion a nation's character and to
deepen a nation's piety." They have been sung, Mr.
Lewis goes on to say, by the shepherd on moor and
mountain, by the blacksmith at his anvil, by the miner
underground, by the milkmaid of an early morning, by
the mother beside the cradle, by the funeral procession
accompanying the dead to the long home, by the young
in their hour of temptation and the veteran in his failing
strength, and by the family of the Lord Christ at the
breaking of the bread in His house. " His hymns became the sacred ballads of the nation. As Luther sang
Germany into Protestantism, so did Williams sing the
Wales of the eighteenth century into piety."

SOME POINTS FOR DISCUSSION

1. The writer of this study is quite out of sympathy
with any movement to revive the name " Jehovah " in
everyday use. And he hopes that the rendering " Je-

hovah is my shepherd " (Ps. 23 : 1) in what is called the
" American Standard Bible " may never become the
standard of our nurseries and schools. As a title of God,
the Hebrew word rendered " Jehovah " seems to belong
exclusively to His people of an older time. It is archaic
and unfamiliar to our Christian habits of speech; and
to introduce it into the Twenty-third Psalm seems to
disconnect the Psalm from our present-day life. But
in this particular hymn the case is quite different. The
poet is trying to recreate the Old Testament atmosphere,
and is employing the journey of the Children of Israel
as a symbol of the Christian life. He almost makes us
feel ourselves a part of the marching host, and the
imagination without an effort thinks of God as Jehovah.

To the writer the phrase " Great Jehovah " here used
has also the surreptitious attraction of a patriotic sug-
gestion; for he finds himself unable to read or sing the
first line without a momentary vision of Ethan Allen
knocking at the door of Fort Ticonderoga and demand-
ing its surrender " In the name of the Great Jehovah
and the Continental Congress."

2. Garrett Horder, the English hymnologist, twice
says in his Hymn Lover that Newman's " Lead, kindly
Light " has almost supplanted " Guide me, O Thou
Great Jehovah." Does this remark tally with our own
observation and experience?

If so, we may remember that Cardinal Newman was
well aware that Dykes's tune had carried his verses into
popularity. And we may well ask if Williams' hymn is
not in need of a deeply felt, elevated, and melodious
tune that will fitly mate with the words. If the hymn
is a little rough, it is not more so than a marching song
ought to be. It is strong and full of feeling and dra-

207   Trust.

Caersalem. M. 8.7.4.   Alaw Gymreig

1

mf Arglwydd, arwain trwy'r anialwch
    Fi, bererin gwael ei wedd,
Nad oes ynof nerth na bywyd,
    Fel yn gorwedd yn y bedd:
cres   Hollalluog
    Ydyw'r un a'm cwyd i'r lan.

1

mf Guide me, O Thou Great Jehovah,
    Pilgrim through this barren land;
p I am weak (*cres*) but Thou art mighty,
    Hold me with Thy powerful hand:
f   Bread of heaven,
    Feed me now and evermore.

THE HYMN AS SET IN THE HYMNAL OF THE CALVINISTIC
METHODIST CHURCH

(Note that the fifth line is sung three times.)

matic force. It wants a tune with a thrill in it. Of the tunes provided in *The Hymnal revised*, Lowell Mason's " Oliphant " begins impressively, but soon goes all to pieces; Viner's " Dismissal " is easy to sing, but does not appeal to the imagination and the feelings as the words do. It seems as if their true setting were yet to seek. But might not our search end happily with the tune " Caersalem," here printed? It is the tune to which the original hymn is sung in Wales itself. The Welsh people have understood it better than we have. We have thought of it as timid and pathetic; they have thought of it as resolute and confident. And in their tune we hear the trumpeters at the head of the marching host sounding forth the clear call of faith, and can catch the response from every quickened heart,

> " I am weak, but Thou are mighty,
>   Hold me with Thy powerful hand."

3. In translating his hymn for Lady Huntingdon's college, Williams added a fourth verse, which reads:

> " Musing on my habitation,
>   Musing on my heav'nly home,
> Fills my soul with holy longings:
>   Come, my Jesus, quickly come;
>   Vanity is all I see;
>   Lord, I long to be with Thee! "

That the addition spoils the hymn is perhaps hardly a topic for discussion. It is as if the new verse said, " I was not really marching in the open: only meditating here in my study."

4. What is the meaning of " Death of deaths and hell's Destruction "? And should " Destruction " be capitalized? Was Mr. Horder, whom we have already referred

to, justified in saying that the hymn is " disfigured by the unpoetic line, ' Death of deaths and hell's destruction ' " ? The phrase seems certainly to have worried a good many people who either did not understand it or else did not like it. The hymnal of the American Methodists has cut the line out and substituted " Bear me through the swelling current."

VIII

LORD, I AM THINE, ENTIRELY THINE

THE TEXT OF THE HYMN

1   Lord, I am Thine, entirely Thine,
Purchased and saved by blood Divine;
With full consent Thine I would be,
And own Thy sovereign right in me.

2   Grant one poor sinner more a place
Among the children of Thy grace;
A wretched sinner lost to God,
But ransomed by Emmanuel's blood.

3   Thine would I live, Thine would I die,
Be Thine through all eternity:
The vow is past beyond repeal;
Now will I set the solemn seal.

4   Here, at that cross where flows the blood
That bought my guilty soul for God,
Thee my new Master now I call,
And consecrate to Thee my all.

Rev. Samuel Davies. Published 1769

NOTE: The hymn was written in Virginia before 1759, but first printed in Dr. Gibbons' London hymn book after Davies' death (1769). The four verses given above are taken from that book: three other verses there found are quoted under "Some Points for Discussion."

THE BEGINNINGS OF HYMN SINGING AMONG AMERICAN PRESBYTERIANS

Whitefield, in his zeal to spread the great revival, made no more of the long voyage to the American colonies than of crossing the border into Wales. Seven times he came, and on his seventh missionary tour died of exhaustion in the home of the Presbyterian pastor at Newburyport, Massachusetts, and was buried beneath the Presbyterian church there. An elaborate cenotaph stands foursquare beside the pulpit, and in the crypt beneath they still show you Whitefield's skull and bones within the glass lid of his coffin, shrined like " the relics " of a saint.

Sitting in the church one Sunday of the summer of 1922 the writer tried to picture those wonderful evangelistic tours of the great preacher: the posting from town to town without rest; the stir of arrival with the eager greetings of his sympathizers pressing close, and from the background cold looks, even occasionally a stone; the quickly gathering throng so soon under the spell of his oratory, sometimes so wrought upon that their cries of distress almost drowned that marvelous voice; the flames of religious excitement rising higher and spreading from place to place into a conflagration that seemed to cover the land. For his heart-searching gospel was a sword rather than a message of peace. It " set a man at variance against his father, and the daughter against her mother " and disrupted the households of faith. Most of the edifices of his own Church of England and many of other denominations shut their doors against him; and the Presbyterian Church was rent into two rival and contentious synods, the one of his supporters, the other of his opponents. It mattered little about the closing of the churches, for no building could hold the throngs, no opposition could quench the flames of the revival that spread into a " Great Awakening " which changed the face of American religion; most of all, perhaps, the face of American Presbyterianism. Presbyterians of our time seem hardly aware of the influence of Whitefield in unmaking and remaking their Church.

Sitting that day in the Newburyport church the writer looked at Whitefield's monument, but it seemed to him that the hymn books in every pew were an even greater monument. For it was that " Great Awakening " which turned the Presbyterian Church in America from a Psalm singing into a hymn singing Church. They were still conscientiously singing the old metrical Psalms (" Rous's Version " mostly) when Whitefield came and stirred men's hearts to the depths with his impassioned gospel. To such overcharged feelings singing affords a natural relief. But both preacher and hearers felt that this new preaching and the old metrical Psalmody did not fit. As Whitefield and his helpers made the cross to shine before men's eyes, their hearts demanded songs that caught and reflected the glory of that cross. Wherever the revival spread, a spontaneous movement began to substitute the evangelical Psalms and hymns of Dr. Watts for the familiar Psalm versions. In the Presbyterian churches that movement began early. It met violent opposition and roused that bitter " Psalmody Controversy " which makes one of the epochs of that Church's history. But it never halted until, after years of strife and even disruption, it had borne down the opposition of " the Psalm singers " and made that

Church the hymn singing body it is to-day. We who love hymns as one of God's best gifts might well pause to remember how hardly our fathers won for us the right to sing them. For that is true of all denominations that bear the impress of Calvin's hand.

THE FIRST HYMNS OF AMERICAN PRESBY-TERIANISM

The hymn we are studying is one of the landmarks of the movement just described. It was written by Samuel Davies, the most brilliant of Presbyterian clergymen in the colonies. He was among the first to chafe under the yoke of the old Psalmody and on his own responsibility to introduce human hymns into his services. He was the earliest Presbyterian hymn writer in the colonies. More than that, he was the earliest American hymn writer of any denomination who wrote hymns still kept in our hymn books and sung by our congregations.

The story of the hymn takes us into Virginia. And we may think of Virginia as the colony most nearly a reproduction of eighteenth century England — in its laws and institutions, its moral conditions and social prejudices. Among other things the English Church was established and rigorously upheld both by law and custom. It was bad form socially to be a dissenter, and unlawful for dissenters to meet for worship. When Whitefield came he was received as a minister of the Church of England, but (perhaps for that reason) his work there was less effective than elsewhere.

It seems to have been a " one-eyed Robinson " who kindled the spark of revival. And a few of " the awakened," who found no help in religion as established, began about 1743 to meet in the home of Samuel Morris to listen to his reading of Whitefield's printed sermons. Similar gatherings began in other houses, and it was eventually determined to build meeting-houses in which the gospel might be freely preached.

The "Newly awakened in Hanover County" put themselves under the care of the "Newside Presbyterians," as Whitefield's supporters were called. But Church and State took alarm. The court demanded the reasons for absence from the church services, and the Governor issued an order against the meetings of the "New Lights." While their trials were still pending the Presbytery of Newcastle, Delaware, ordained young Samuel Davies with a view to shepherding these new congregations. He succeeded in getting from the General Court of Virginia a special license to preach to them, and was wonderfully successful with two extreme classes, the gentlemen and the black slaves. He was so touched by the singing of the latter that he sent to England for supplies of Watts's "Psalms and Hymns," as he felt those warmer evangelical strains made more appeal to the emotional blacks than the old metrical Psalm versions. To Davies, as to most of the preachers who favored "human hymns," the great office of the hymn was to enforce the appeal of the sermon. When he could not find a hymn in Watts suitable to the sermon in hand, he wrote one of his own in Watts's style and manner. His hymns were composed in the glow of sermon-writing, and put into verse the points he most wished to impress upon the heart and conscience. He gave them out line by line to be sung after the sermon, and sometimes when requested to print a particular sermon, he printed the appropriate hymn also at the end.

SAMUEL DAVIES

Most of his hymns, and of course most of his sermons also, remained unprinted during his life. But Davies, while in England on a mission to raise money for Princeton College, had formed a warm friendship with Dr. Thomas Gibbons, an influential pastor in London, and a friend by the way both of Dr. Watts and Lady Huntingdon. In 1757, Davies, getting up from a dangerous illness, wrote Dr. Gibbons that he wanted to be useful after he was dead, and had put in his will an order to transmit all his sermon manuscripts to Dr. Gibbons, to publish such as might promise to do good. And so, after Davies' death in 1761, his manuscript sermons (with the appended hymns) were boxed up in Princeton and made the long voyage to England in safety.

Dr. Gibbons got ready enough sermons to fill three volumes, and printed them in 1765. They were so successful that he published other volumes later, and all have often been reprinted since. In his preface he spoke of the hymns and expressed a purpose of printing them also in the future. This he did in a hymn book of his own, *Hymns adapted to Divine Worship*, published in 1769: sixteen of them in all with this note, " The Pieces in the following Miscellany ascribed to the Rev. Mr. DAVIES, were found in his Manuscripts intrusted with the Editor." So it was that eight years after Davies had been laid to rest at Princeton his hymns were given to the world in far-off London, as the last kindly office of the hand of friendship.

Dr. Gibbons' hymn book reached a small circle, but Dr. John Rippon gave a wider circulation to seven of Davies' hymns he took from it into his popular Baptist *Selection* of 1787. The particular hymn we are now studying he spoiled by cutting it down to two verses and changing the first line to a question, " Lord, am I Thine, entirely Thine? " Perhaps that is why it is so little used in England. The one best known there is " Great God of wonders! all Thy ways," which has been found in over a hundred English hymn books. Rippon's mutilated text of the present hymn was copied into several early books in this country. But when the Presbyterian Church in the U.S.A. ventured to make its own *Psalms and Hymns* in 1830, " Lord, I am Thine " was included as Dr. Gibbons had printed it. It has been a standard hymn ever since and is familiarly used also by the Reformed, Baptist, Congregationalist, Methodist, and Lutheran Churches. In how many hearts is it tenderly associated with the hour of self-surrender and the scene of the first Communion!

THE AUTHOR OF THE HYMN

Some twenty-three miles below Wilmington, in Newcastle County, Delaware, stands a colonial Presbyterian church known as " Old Drawyer's," which is still the shrine of a yearly pious pilgrimage. On a farm not more than twelve miles away Samuel Davies was born, November 3, 1723, of plain Welsh parents. He was educated at the academy of Samuel Blair at Fagg's Manor, who also prepared him for his ordination by the Presbytery of Newcastle in February, 1747.

Davies' work in Virginia was made difficult at first by a physical breakdown supposed to indicate a hopeless stage of consumption, and to this was added the sorrow of a young wife's death. But he went bravely on, often preaching by day when so ill that attendants had to sit up with him by night. He recovered his health, and it was probably on account of his persuasive eloquence that he was chosen to go abroad with Gilbert Tennent on behalf of Princeton College.

Coming back in February, 1755, he found the Virginia settlements greatly agitated at the aggressions of the French and Indian alliance. The alarm spread when, in July, the little army of General Braddock sent out to capture Fort Duquesne was defeated, with only a remnant saved by the courage of George Washington, then a youth of twenty-three. The always fervid preacher now became a passionate patriot, arousing Virginia by his call to arms.

It was in printing a sermon preached to Captain Overton's Company of Independent Volunteers in August of the same year that Davies added the prophetic footnote so often quoted, " I may point out to the public that heroic youth, Col. Washington, whom I cannot but hope Providence has hitherto preserved, in so signal a manner, for some important service to his country."

Three years later Davies was called to succeed the famous Jonathan Edwards as president of Princeton College. He declined and only under the pressure of a re-election consented to leave his beloved Virginia. He took to Princeton great gifts and a great reputation, but had filled the office hardly more than eighteen months when he caught a cold to which he succumbed, dying on February 4, 1761, at the age of thirty-six. His grave now makes one of the famous Presidents' Row at Princeton, where he lies next to Jonathan Edwards.

Davies was not only the most brilliant but quite the most engaging figure of colonial Presbyterianism. Makemie may have been a greater administrator, but one

The following Answer was finished July 4, 1755: A.D. while the Author was pursuing it among a few Friends, in order to review their remarks, before it should go to the Press, the Country took an alarm, & struck into a Consternation, with the News of General Braddock's Defeat. He therefore took the Publication of it unseasonable at that Time, & let it lie by him, for some months, designing to publish it, when the Attention of the Public should not be so much engaged. But during this Delay, Mr. Bell Alexr. died, & then he felt the Publication entirely improper, left he should seem to insult the Memory of the dead, for which he had a sincere regard, or to triumph without an Antagonist. Decem. 23, 1755.

PREFACE FROM A MANUSCRIPT WORK OF DAVIES

imagines him a little rough. Gilbert Tennent in early
life was possibly an equally effective preacher, but he
had a vein of hardness and censoriousness. His later
preaching did not sustain his reputation, while even now
when we read Davies' printed sermons we catch the light
and feel the glow. They far surpass the printed sermons
of Whitefield himself, which indeed make poor reading.
Makemie, Tennent, Davies — all three were God's am-
bassadors, but Davies had the gracious manners and
social accomplishments of the trained diplomat. He had
the inscrutable quality we call " charm," that wins the
admiration of strangers, and the deeper qualities of
mind and heart that won from his friends the fullness of
affection so frankly written in all their reminiscences
of him.

SOME POINTS FOR DISCUSSION

1. Dr. Gibbons did not tell us to which of the manuscript sermons that came into his hands this hymn was
appended. It seems to fit the one he printed as " XXXI,
Dedication to God argued from Redeeming Mercy," from
I Cor. 6:19, 20. The preacher enters God's claim to
all his hearers have and are; their solemn business
at the Lord's Table is " to yield themselves to God, and
seal their indenture to be His." He asks them to follow
while he proposes the terms of the transaction, and, if
they consent, to " rise and crowd round the table of their
Lord, and there annex their solemn seals and acknowledge it to be their act and deed." And this is the " con-
tract ": " Lord, here is a poor sinner, thy creature redeemed by the blood of thy Son, that has long been a
slave to other masters, and withheld from thee thy just

and dear-bought property; here, Lord, I would now, freely and without reserve, devote and surrender myself, my soul and body, and my all to thee, to be universally and for ever thine. And let the omnipotent God, let angels and men, be witness to the engagement."

Does there seem much room to doubt that the hymn was written to be used at the Communion service that was to follow this particular sermon?

2. But at what date? In *The Hymnal revised* the footnote gives it as " published in 1769 "; and that is the only date we have. The sermon was preached in Virginia (before July, 1759, that is to say), is addressed to black and white, freeman and slave, and refers to a possible persecution even unto death. May not that suggest as a date the time of the French and Indian aggressions and the dread that the conquering French might establish the Roman Catholic discipline in the colony?

3. Dr. Gibbons printed this hymn in seven verses. The familiar abridgment into four verses may perhaps be of some practical advantage. But the whole hymn is needed to show its full relation to Sermon XXXI. To obtain this, insert after the first verse in *The Hymnal revised*,

> II. Here, Lord, my Flesh, my Soul, my All
> I yield to Thee beyond Recall;
> Accept thine own so long withheld,
> Accept what I so freely yield!

after the third verse,

> V. Be thou the Witness of my Vow,
> Angels and Men attest it too,
> That to thy Board I now repair,
> And seal the sacred Contract there.

and after the fourth verse,

> VII. Do Thou assist a feeble Worm
> The great Engagement to perform:
> Thy Grace can full Assistance lend,
> And on that Grace I dare depend.

4. Just what is the effect upon this hymn of the alteration made by Dr. Rippon by which the affirmation of its first line becomes the question, " Lord, am I Thine, entirely Thine? "'

THE WHITEFIELD MONUMENT
AT NEWBURYPORT

IX

SWEET THE MOMENTS, RICH IN BLESSING

THE TEXT OF THE HYMN

1 Sweet the moments, rich in blessing,
   Which before the cross I spend;
Life and health and peace possessing
   From the sinner's dying Friend.

2 Here I'll sit, for ever viewing
   Mercy's streams in streams of blood;
Precious drops, my soul bedewing,
   Plead and claim my peace with God.

3 Truly blessèd is this station,
   Low before His cross to lie,
While I see Divine compassion
   Pleading in His languid eye.

4 Love and grief my heart dividing,
   With my tears His feet I'll bathe;
Constant still in faith abiding,
   Life deriving from His death.

5 For Thy sorrows we adore Thee,
   For the griefs that wrought our peace;
Gracious Saviour, we implore Thee,
   In our hearts Thy love increase.

The Hon. and Rev. Walter Shirley, 1770: based upon
an earlier (1757) hymn by the Rev. James Allen.

NOTE: The first four verses as here given are taken from Shirley's hymn book of 1770; with such changes as will appear by comparison with his text hereafter quoted in full. The fifth verse was added to the hymn in the Rev. Messrs. Cooke and Denton's *Church Hymnal* of 1853.

In our study of " Guide me, O Thou Great Jehovah," we met, somewhat casually, the Lady Selina Shirley, by marriage Countess of Huntingdon. And she, beyond a doubt, is the proper person to introduce her first cousin, the Honorable and Reverend Walter Shirley, whose skillful hand gave to our present hymn its familiar shape. Especially so, as it was written to be sung in her own chapels.

" HER LADYSHIP'S CONNEXION "

After a dangerous illness and a deep experience Lady Huntingdon " turned Methodist," as the phrase was, to the dismay of her friends. " I thank your Ladyship," wrote the Duchess of Buckingham, " for the information concerning the Methodist preachers; their doctrines are most repulsive, and strongly tinctured with impertinence and disrespect towards their superiors, in perpetually endeavoring to level all ranks, and do away with all distinctions. It is monstrous to be told, that you have a heart as sinful as the common wretches that crawl on the earth. This is highly offensive and insulting; and I cannot but wonder that your Ladyship should relish any sentiments so much at variance with high rank and good breeding." Her Ladyship, on the other hand, persuaded many of her friends, even the Duchess sometimes, to go with her to the Methodist meetings, and gathered more of them to hear Methodist preachers in her own London

" THE REV'D MR. SHIRLEY "

drawing-room. With her zeal and influence she gave a
new turn to the great revival. She introduced it into
aristocratic circles. " Methodism," the cynical Horace
Walpole used to complain, " is becoming quite fashionable."

When the split came in 1741, Lady Huntingdon adhered to Whitefield. Beginning as his commissary, she
soon took the field in person as commander in chief of
his forces. Whitefield needed such a patron. John Wesley was a master hand at organizing; and a world-wide
Methodist Church is his monument. Whitefield was a
great preacher, and just that. He could make converts,
but for organizing and molding these same converts into
a permanent body of Christian workers he had no gifts.

Just here Lady Huntingdon took hold. By birth and
marriage she was a great lady, with full sense of her high
social position. She was also a great woman, of the
" modern " type: a born executive, indifferent to conven-
tionalities, bent on getting results, deeply religious, with
an autocratic will. After her husband's death she had
houses and an ample income at her command, and was
generous to the point of stripping herself of all but bare
necessities. She paid for her first chapel by selling her
jewels.

She built many other chapels in different parts of
England, and joined them as a " connexion " of which
she was the head. She sought out Calvinistic clergymen
to preach from their pulpits the gospel as she believed it,
and when the supply failed, founded that theological
school at Trevecca whose " young collegians " we heard
singing " Guide me, O Thou Great Jehovah." She retained the Prayer Book services in her chapels, but the
bright and hearty hymn singing she set up in place of

the droning of metrical Psalms in parish churches, proved a great attraction. She had learned from the Wesleys and Whitefield what evangelical songs had done for the revival. She loved them and sang them and became one of the influences that were gradually spreading the singing of " hymns of human composure." In the end her chapels got her into trouble with the Church authorities, who liked neither her independence nor her gospel, and in her old age she had to organize her forces as a dissenting body outside the Church of England — " Lady Huntingdon's Connexion."

THE STORY OF THE HYMN

The story circles about Lady Huntingdon, and involves a number of people. There was first the Rev. Benjamin Ingham, one of the original Methodists, who went to Georgia with the Wesleys, and is said to have been too handsome for a man. On his return he became a successful evangelist, and formed many " societies " of his converts in his native Yorkshire and thereabouts. In 1741 he married Lady Huntingdon's sister-in-law. " The news I hear from London," wrote Lady Mary Wortley Montague from Rome, " is that Lady Margaret Hastings has disposed of herself to a poor, wandering Methodist preacher." In the year following he deserted the Methodists and joined the Moravian Brethren. After some years he changed his views again, and left the Moravians. But instead of joining Lady Huntingdon's Connexion, he formed some thousands of his followers into a brand-new denomination, the Inghamite Connexion.

Now it would never do for Inghamites to go on singing Moravian hymns, or to fall back on those of the Methodists. And so some of Ingham's helpers tried their hand at hymn writing. The chief of these was one James Allen, a young Yorkshireman who had been intended for the ministry of the established Church, but who was converted under Ingham's preaching, and broke off a college course at the University of Cambridge to become one of his preachers. Allen wrote more than sixty hymns, and these, with others by his colleagues, he printed in 1757 for the Inghamite Connexion. He called his book *A Collection of Hymns for the use of those that seek, and those that have Redemption in the Blood of Christ;* but it is more generally referred to as " The Kendal Hymn Book." Naturally enough, these new hymns retained a good many of the Moravian peculiarities. Some that dealt with the person of our Lord had the same unpleasant sensuous flavor that John Wesley protested against.

The Inghamite collection is not attractive. If there were no better "hymns of human composure" than these, most people would gladly go back to metrical versions of the Psalms. But for a while they appealed to the ecstatic feelings of the Inghamites. And only for a while could Ingham hold his followers together. He could not even hold James Allen. That good man at last " saw the light " and became a " Glassite." " My eyes," he said, " were never fully opened till the latter end of October, 1762. How am I now ashamed of my preaching, and the hymn book I was concerned in printing! Almost every page puts me to the blush." In the end this honest but erratic seeker for truth found such measure of church unity as he was capable of by building a private chapel on his Yorkshire estate, and ministering there undisturbed until his death in 1804.

60

8. Oh! that in heart none may draw back;
So shall we ne'er his favours lack,
But feel them ever new:
Press on, and we the prize shall win;
Unfold to him each grief within;
He's ever ever true.

LIV.

WHILE my Jesus I'm possessing,
Great's the happiness I know;
While him ___ I am caressing,
Sweetest odours round me flow:
Happy I'm in his embraces,
Proving all his kisses sweet;
Singing never-ceasing praises,
Mary-like before his feet.

2. Oh! how happy are the moments,
Which I here in transport spend;
Life deriving from his torments,
Who remains the sinner's Friend:
Here I'll sit for ever viewing
How the blood flows from each vein;
Ev'ry stream, my soul bedewing,
Mortifies the carnal flame.

3. Really blessed is the portion
Destin'd me by sov'reign grace;
Still to view divine compassion
In the Saviour's bruised face:
'Tis my fixed resolution,
Jesus Christ my Lord to love;
At his feet to fix my station,
Nor from thence a hair's breadth move.

4. Here it is I find my heaven,
While upon my Lamb I gaze;
Love I much, I've more forgiven;
I'm a miracle of grace:

61

Fill'd with sinner-like contrition,
With my tears his feet I'll bathe;
Happy in the sweet fruition
Of my Saviour's painful death.

5. From his pierc'd and wounded body
Issu'd streams of sacred gore;
From his hands and feet so bloody
Flow'd a med'cine for each sore:
From his side, that fountain precious,
Pardons with the blood did flow;
This to taste is most delicious,
Causing all within to glow.

6. May I still enjoy this feeling,
In all need to Jesus go;
Prove his wounds each day more healing,
And from hence salvation draw:
May I have the spirit's unction
Filling me with holy shame;
Still retain a close connection
With the person of the Lamb.

LV.

JESUS, how glorious was the day,
When Thou didst my release proclaim
Sweetly I sung the hours away;
I sung salvation thro' thy name.

2. I wonder'd how the careless crowd
Senseless could sleep away their day;
So strong thy love in my heart flow'd,
Such solid peace it did convey.

3. Close with thy flock I was combin'd,
Nought could my heart from their's divide;
By blood's cementing power join'd,
With them I could have liv'd and dy'd.

4. Beneath thy word refresh'd I stood;
Thy word to me with power came;

THE HYMN AS JAMES ALLEN WROTE IT

Among Allen's contributions to the hymn book of 1757 was one of six double verses, beginning

"While my Jesus I'm possessing."

We know it is his because he marked it with his initials in his own copy of the book. It was far from being good; and when the Inghamites were dispersed, and the little book was disowned by its editor, that hymn would seem to have been finally buried out of sight.

But now the Hon. and Rev. Walter Shirley comes on to play his part. He was born in 1725 of noble blood: a younger brother of the notorious Earl Ferrers, who threatened his wife, murdered his steward, and was hanged after a trial by the House of Lords. Shirley was drawn into the revival movement through his connection with Lady Huntingdon. He became one of her preachers, although he remained in the Church of England all his life, with a parish in Ireland. But his evangelical theology and his revival preaching kept him in bad odor with his bishop and fellow clergymen.

Lady Huntingdon trusted him, and seems to have given him charge of the hymnological department of her Connexion; but it was under her own eye. She attached great importance to the character of the hymns. If she did not write any (this is uncertain), she saw to it that none was sung in her chapels of which she did not approve. For the editing of her special collections she depended upon Mr. Shirley. It was in the 1770 edition of *The Collection of Hymns sung in the Countess of Huntingdon's Chapel* [at Bath] that Shirley printed the hymn we know so well as " Sweet the moments, rich in blessing." Like a careful editor he had gone over other books to find available material, even the Inghamite book. By comparing Shirley's verses with the facsimile of Allen's original as here given, we can see for our-selves how he found the hymn embedded in Allen's mate-rial, just as a sculptor sees a symmetrical figure embedded in the rough and shapeless mass of marble. He had a keen eye and a cunning hand, certainly. He made what for all practical purposes is a new hymn.

As we have before us the full text as Allen wrote it, it may be interesting to have also the full text as Shirley rewrote it:

> Sweet the Moments rich in Blessing
>   Which before the Cross I spend;
> Life and Health, and Peace possessing,
>   From the Sinner's dying Friend.
> Here I'll sit for ever viewing
>   Mercy's Streams in Streams of Blood;
> Precious Drops my soul bedewing
>   Plead and claim my Peace with GOD.
>
> Truly blessed is this Station
>   Low before his Cross to lye;
> While I see divine Compassion
>   Floating in his languid Eye.
> Here it is I find my Heaven,
>   While upon the Lamb I gaze;
> Love I much, I've much forgiven,
>   I'm a Miracle of Grace.
>
> Love and Grief my Heart dividing,
>   With my Tears his Feet I'll bathe;
> Constant still in Faith abiding,
>   Life deriving from his Death.
> May I still enjoy this Feeling,
>   In all Need to *Jesus* go;
> Prove his Wounds each Day more healing,
>   And himself more deeply know.

Comparison shows the weak parts of Shirley's compilation to be just those that adhered most closely to Allen's original: the second quatrain of verse two, culminating in that smug line, "I'm a Miracle of Grace," and the last four lines of all, which fail to reach a climax. It was easy for later editors to drop these lines, but to arrange a fitting climax for the whole hymn was another matter. That indeed was wanting until two English clergymen, Messrs. Cooke and Denton, in their *Church Hymnal* of 1853, added the fine lines:

> For Thy Sorrows we adore Thee —
> For the Griefs that wrought our peace —
> Gracious Saviour! we implore Thee,
> In our hearts Thy love increase.

SOME POINTS FOR DISCUSSION

1. This is called by hymnologists a Good Friday hymn. Until recent years no notice was taken of that day in Presbyterian and some other churches. The observance of Good Friday came about as a consequence of the observance of Easter Day. The writer can remember when Easter itself was ignored in Presbyterian churches. But when the celebration of Easter became firmly established, the question began to be asked: Is it not a strange thing for an evangelical Church, that puts the emphasis upon the cross, to celebrate the anniversary of the resurrection and ignore the anniversary of the crucifixion? It was an awkward question. And when once asked, there could be only one logical answer. The recognition of Good Friday has been to some extent forced upon the churches in those states which had made it a legal holiday. It is better certainly to keep the anniversary as a holy day,

with religious services, than as a Roman holiday given over to public amusements. It is, however, likely that the propriety of recognizing the day in Presbyterian churches may be a topic for discussion for years to come.

It is also a subject for discussion, whether the present hymn might not well be reserved for use on some such special occasion, when our feelings are moved by the pathos of the cross. Is it not perhaps too tender in feeling to justify the familiar use it has had in everyday social services?

2. In the text, as printed in *The Hymnal revised,* there is a striking change when we pass from the " I " of the four Shirley verses to the " we " of the Cooke and Denton verse. Much has been written as to whether our congregational songs should have the " I " and " my " of an individual singer or the " we " and " our " of the congregation as a common body. And this hymn suggests an answer. It is as if each singer came alone to the cross, and there laid low his heart, all alone with Christ. And as if all the singers then arose and stood together at the cross in one common outburst of praise and adoration.

3. There are few meaner things in this world than plagiarism. Plagiarism is the stealing of the products of another's brain, and giving them forth as our own. It is good, therefore, in tracing these verses to the little known original of the obscure James Allen, to remember that Shirley was quite innocent of plagiarism. He neither signed them nor claimed them as his own. His only ambition was to furnish his cousin's chapels with good hymns. It is not even possible to say how many of these were written by himself.

X

ROCK OF AGES, CLEFT FOR ME

THE TEXT OF THE HYMN

1 Rock of Ages, cleft for me,
   Let me hide myself in Thee;
   Let the water and the blood,
   From Thy riven side which flowed,
   Be of sin the double cure,
   Cleanse me from its guilt and power.

2 Not the labors of my hands
   Can fulfil Thy law's demands;
   Could my zeal no respite know,
   Could my tears for ever flow,
   All for sin could not atone;
   Thou must save, and Thou alone.

3 Nothing in my hand I bring,
   Simply to Thy cross I cling;
   Naked, come to Thee for dress,
   Helpless, look to Thee for grace;
   Foul, I to the fountain fly;
   Wash me, Saviour, or I die.

4 While I draw this fleeting breath,
   When my eyelids close in death,
   When I soar to worlds unknown,
   See Thee on Thy judgment throne,
   Rock of Ages, cleft for me,
   Let me hide myself in Thee.

Rev. Augustus M. Toplady, in *The Gospel Magazine* for March, 1776

NOTE: The text is that of Toplady's own *Psalms and Hymns* of 1776, except in the second line of the last verse, whose alteration is explained under " Some Points for Discussion."

" Rock of Ages " was written by Augustus Montague
Toplady, one of the converts of the same Methodist revival that produced " Jesus, Lover of my soul." But
he had lost his sympathy with Wesley's doctrinal views,
turned his back on Methodism, and become a Church of
England clergyman. Two things, however, he had kept
in his heart — the fervor of the Methodists and their
love for songs that had the glow of the gospel in them.
He not only wrote hymns of his own but he joined a
little group of men who were doing their best to win a
place for hymn singing in the Church of England itself.

A NEW ATTACK UPON THE OLD PSALM SINGING

In our third study we saw how young Isaac Watts chal-
lenged the old custom of singing metrical Psalms, and
won the hearts of the Independent congregations with
his own very human hymns. In our fourth study we saw
how the Wesley brothers followed in the next generation
with their gospel songs, and made these a great power in
the Methodist Revival.

With the Independents singing Watts's hymns and the
Methodists singing the Wesleys', it might seem that the
" hymn of human composure " had come to its own in
England. But not yet. The great established Church
clung to the old Psalms. Most of its bishops and clergy
cared little for the Independents and despised the Methodists as fanatics. The thing they most dreaded in religion was " enthusiasm," which they regarded as bad
form. As the Methodist singing became clamorous, they
felt the greater dislike for hymns as the particular
vehicle of this vulgar " enthusiasm." The good and

great Dr. Johnson, a churchman of the better sort, notes
in his diary that on Easter Day, 1764, he gave a crown
to a poor girl he met in church, although he saw a hymn
book in her hand. He was pluming himself on a charitable impulse that could even surmount the prejudice
against hymn singers.

But enthusiasm is a contagious thing, and even the
lethargic Church of England could not escape it altogether. We have already seen how Lady Huntingdon
succumbed, and how, when the doctrinal split came in
1741, she took charge of Whitefield's forces, and began
to stir up a revival in the Church itself. The little group
of clergy who shared Whitefield's Calvinistic views and
sympathized with his revival measures, were content for
a while to preach and work under the great lady's aus-
pices. But when she became a dissenter, most of them
kept their places in the established Church and gradually formed an Evangelical or Low Church Party to carry
on the revival within the bounds of the Church. They
protested against being called Methodists, but for a
good while they protested in vain. What seemed to
outsiders to give them away was their revival
preaching, and especially their addiction to the new and
strange practice of singing human hymns in place of the
long established Psalm singing. For with one exception,
these leaders were all agreed that evangelical religion has
the right to express itself in evangelical songs. In 1753,
Whitefield had made his own hymn book for use in the
revival services of his London Tabernacle. Seven years
later the Rev. Martin Madan followed with another for
use in his chapel at the Lock Hospital. It was a private
chapel and not a parish church, or else Mr. Madan would
have got into trouble, just as Mr. Wesley did at Savannah,

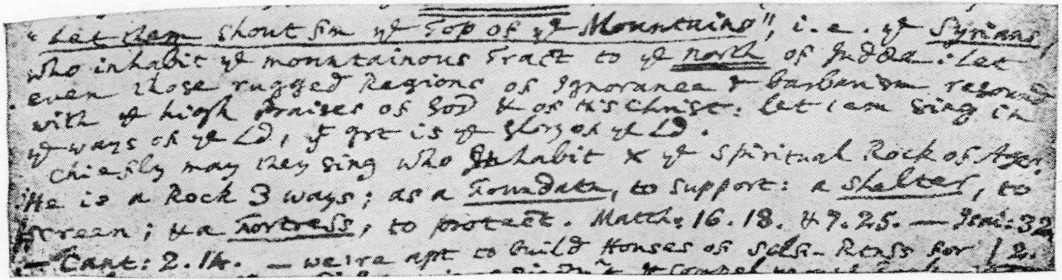
"Let them shout from ye Top of ye Mountains", i.e. ye Syrians,
who inhabit ye mountainous tract to ye north of Judea: let
even those rugged Regions of Ignorance & barbarism resound
with ye high praises of God & of his Christ: let them sing in
ye ways of ye Ld, yt grt is ye glory of ye Ld.
Chiefly may they sing who inhabit ye spiritual Rock of Ages.
He is a Rock 3 ways; as a Foundation, to support: a Shelter, to
screen; & a Fortress, to protect. Matth: 16.18. & 7.25. — Isai: 32.2.
— Cant: 2.14. — we're apt to build Houses of Self-Riss for

AUTOGRAPH LINES FROM A SERMON OF TOPLADY

for introducing unauthorized hymns into the Church service.

To this Evangelical Party in the Church of England Mr. Toplady attached himself as one of its younger members. And in 1776 he, too, printed a collection of *Psalms and Hymns* for his Orange Street Chapel in London. It was his " Declaration of Independence " from the fetters of the old Psalmody. It was even more memorable as the first hymn book in which his own " Rock of Ages " appeared and thus began its remarkable career. Toplady wrote other hymns that have been widely sung. But " Rock of Ages " is to-day in more church hymnals than is any other English hymn. And in the opinion of many judges it is the greatest hymn in the language. Its warmth of feeling and fervor of devotion, with a certain note of solemnity like the rhythmic pealing of deep-toned bells, have made an abiding impression upon millions of human hearts.

THE AUTHOR OF THE HYMN

It is an odd coincidence that as Charles Wesley was born in the year in which Watts printed " There is a land of pure delight," so Toplady was born in the year in which the Wesleys printed " Jesu, Lover of my soul."

He was born in the English village of Farnham on November 4, 1740. His father, a major in the army, died in the field within a few months of the birth of the son, who was left to the abundant love of the widow. He was a white-faced, fragile, neurotic child, mentally and spiritually so precocious as to be abnormal. He remarked in his diary: " I am now arrived at the age of eleven years. I praise God I can remember no dreadful crime: and not to me but to the Lord be the glory. Amen. It is now past eight o'clock, and now I think fit to withdraw, but yet my heart is so full of divine and holy raptures, that a sheet of paper could not contain my writings." Self-conscious, proud, and passionate, he composes a daily prayer to be kept from quarreling with his schoolmates.

AUGUSTUS M. TOPLADY

At twelve he is writing sermons and preaching to those who will hear; and his mother embroiders for him a pulpit fall. She dotes on him, and is bringing him up, the grandmother thinks, to be a scourge to her. His uncle and aunt cannot make him out and frankly detest him. These critical relatives, one by one, the child pillories in his diary. Aunt Betsy, for example, " is so vastly quarrelsome; in short, she is so fractious, and captious, and insolent, that she is unfit for human so-

ciety." A boy who fails to appear at the hour appointed
becomes "the dishonourable Norreys." A woman who
"said I am a second Timothy" fared better, though "I
do not set this down from my vanity." At thirteen he
composes a farce, which he intends to show to the great
Mr. Garrick of Drury Lane. At fourteen he becomes a
writer of hymns, and at nineteen publishes a volume of
them.

After his school days in London, Toplady went with
his mother to Ireland, and entered Trinity College, Dublin. One summer day in 1756, at a revival meeting in
an Irish barn, he "was brought nigh to God" under a
sermon by a Methodist preacher, James Morris. He determined to prepare for the ministry. But he then held
to the Arminian theology of Methodism. When he came
to study the Thirty-nine Articles of the Church of England he was surprised to find them Calvinistic, and
thought he would have to seek a sphere in one of the
Arminian sects. Further study brought deep misgiv-
ings, and in great agitation of mind he completely
changed his views. He became an ardent Calvinist, and
as such entered the ministry of the Church of England.

His ministry was to be short. He was curate of Blagdon, in Somerset, in 1762, and of Farley Hungerford two
years later; then vicar of Harpford and Fen Ottery, and
later of Broad Hembury; three obscure villages of
Devon, not far from Exeter. He preached with great
nervous excitement, his flaming spirit set in the frail
candlestick of a diseased body. The seeds of consumption developed — in those days an inevitable doom. He
craved a larger opportunity for his last years. His
friends engaged the Huguenot Chapel in Orange Street,
London, where he preached to great congregations, until

no longer able to mount the pulpit steps. On August
11, 1778, that passionate heart ceased to beat. His body
was buried within the walls of Whitefield's Tabernacle in
Tottenham Court Road.

Toplady lived in a time of theological controversy.
And when he adopted Calvinistic views in his ardent way,
he felt that he had been delivered from a dark pit, in
which John Wesley dwelt as a sort of Jinnee. In a pamphlet of 1769, *The Church of England vindicated from
the charge of Arminianism,* he tried to prove that the
Church was Calvinistic. Henceforward in conversation,
letters, sermons, hymns, tracts, and treatises he spent
himself in setting forth and defending the Calvinistic
doctrine of Election.

The actual quarrel with John Wesley began after Toplady published later in the same year a translation of
Zanchius on Predestination. Wesley printed an abridgment of it for his societies, with a stinging preface of his
own, and at the end an unfair summary professing to
be signed " A—— T——."

Toplady's feelings were outraged by what he called
" Mr. Wesley's lying abridgment " and " forging " of his
signature. He printed *A Letter to the Rev. Mr. John
Wesley,* which in the recklessness of its misjudgment of
a good man, the audacity of its unmerited charges, and
the offensiveness of its language, has never, one likes
to think, had a parallel in religious debate. It was indeed pitiful, if only a burst of sudden passion, or if it
stood alone. But it was followed by *More work for Mr.
John Wesley, an old Fox tarred and feathered,* and by
a hounding of Wesley's name and reputation that ended
only with death.

In his last illness Toplady had himself taken to the

Orange Street Chapel. Some one had started a rumor that he had changed his views and wished to converse with Mr. Wesley. At the end of the sermon preached by another, Toplady's emaciated figure mounted the pulpit steps. He hoped, he said, his last hours " would be much better employed than in conversing with such a man." Were he on his death-bed with a pen in his hand, he " would not strike out a single line " he had written relative to Wesley and his doctrines.

No wonder that Professor J. Ritchie Smith, of Princeton Seminary, should exclaim in his *The Wall and the Gates*, " Is this the author of Rock of Ages ? " and should cite Toplady as a historical illustration of the fact that " orthodoxy covers a multitude of sins in our sight, though it may be itself the worst of sins." The veneration that surrounds Toplady's name in so many books is due to some extent to party spirit. Though not a widely read theologian, he was the clearest brain and the recognized leader on the Calvinistic side in " a hot time," and his followers inevitably glorified him. It is best to say frankly that his combative side deserves the veneration of no Christian. To seek some palliation of Toplady's offense in a morbid body and diseased nerves is right enough. We may try to forgive it, but we cannot, if we are to study " Rock of Ages," forget it, for he has chosen to use the hymn as part of his " case " against Wesley, just as a lawyer annexes an " exhibit " to his brief.

In the meantime the pure and fervid hymn is none the less the gift of God. He is pleased to store His gifts in earthen vessels. Neither a holy sacrament nor a holy hymn is spoiled by any lack of perfect whiteness in the human hand through which it comes.

THE STORY OF THE HYMN

Outside the village of Burrington Combe in Somerset, England, a limestone crag rises some seventy or eighty feet. Down the center is a deep fissure, in whose recesses ferns grow. During July, 1921, some English newspapers announced that a pilgrimage was being organized to visit the spot, as that in which Toplady composed " Rock of Ages, cleft for me." On the Bank Holiday of August following, a great company, estimated at ten thousand, made the pilgrimage, and in the natural amphitheater facing the crag joined in prayer, heard addresses, and sang the hymn. It was a wonderful testimonial to the power of the hymn after a hundred and forty-five years.

The odd feature of the occasion is that no one present could have known that Toplady wrote the hymn there or even had the crag in mind when he did write it. There is a local tradition, apparently not old but carefully fostered, that he was caught one day by a thunderstorm in Burrington Combe, took refuge in the fissure, and there wrote the hymn. No evidence of the truth of the story has ever been produced. It seems more likely that the story grew out of the " cleft for me " in the hymn, rather than that the hymn proceeded from the fissure. Just as in the case of " Jesus, Lover of my soul," the story of the dove taking refuge in Charles Wesley's breast grew out of the line, " Let me to Thy bosom fly."

It is true that the crag is within walking distance of Blagdon Church, where Toplady was curate. But he left there in 1764, and not a line of the hymn is known to exist until October, 1775 — eleven years afterwards.

THE ROCK WHICH LOCAL TRADITION NAMES AS THE INSPI-
RATION OF TOPLADY'S HYMN, "ROCK OF AGES,
CLEFT FOR ME"

The present writer sees little room for doubt that what Toplady actually had before him when he wrote the hymn was a copy of the Wesleys' *Hymns on the Lord's Supper* (1745), of which eleven editions had appeared before the date of the hymn. It was a book Toplady would be sure to examine. And on page eight of the prefatory matter he would find the following passage: " O Rock of *Israel,* Rock of Salvation, Rock struck and cleft for me, let those two Streams of *Blood* and *Water* which once gushed out of Thy side, bring down *Pardon* and *Holiness* into my soul. And let me thirst after them now, as if I stood upon the Mountain whence sprung *this Water;* and near the *Cleft* of that Rock, the Wounds of my Lord, whence gushed this sacred *Blood.*" If anyone questions that we have here the source from which Toplady drew the theme and imagery of the hymn, he may turn to Hymn XXVII of the same book, whose opening is,

" Rock of Israel, cleft for me."

It is not doubt one is likely to feel, but wonder; wonder that Toplady could appropriate these materials and yet write of John Wesley, " I believe him to be the most rancorous hater of the gospel-system, that ever appeared in this island."

We get our first glimpse of the hymn in *The Gospel Magazine* for October, 1775, where, in an article on " Life a Journey," Toplady says: " Yet, if you fall, be humbled; but do not despair. . . . Look to the blood of the covenant; and say to the Lord, from the depth of your heart,

" Rock of Ages, cleft for me,
Let me hide myself in thee!
Foul, I to the fountain fly:
Wash me, Saviour, or I die."

Whether the hymn was completely written out then, we shall never know.

After he became editor of the magazine, Toplady printed in the number for March, 1776, a curious article by " J. F." — aiming to show that England could never pay her national debt. Toplady appended a " spiritual improvement," showing that sinners are in the same case as regards their debt to the moral law. Reckoning one sin to every second, " at ten years old, each of us is chargeable with 315 millions and 36 thousand sins. At twenty, with 630 millions, and 720 thousand," and so on, by decades, till the end of life. " This debt we can never pay. But Christ has redeemed us from the curse of the Law and His Blood cleanseth from all sin. We must bless God the Father for electing us, God the Son for assuming our debts, God the Holy Spirit for His gift of faith in Christ."

Then follow the four verses of the hymn. Unfortunately, even in this mood of exaltation, Toplady cannot overlook John Wesley. And he heads his hymn, *" A living and dying* PRAYER *for the* HOLIEST BELIEVER *in the World."* Possibly that sarcastic phrase, " the holiest believer in the world," did not refer to Wesley in person, but to any follower who thought he exemplified Wesley's doctrine that entire holiness is attainable while in the flesh. Even a perfectionist, perhaps Toplady means, is none too holy to use the words of this hymn.

Toplady, as has been said, included " Rock of Ages " in his collection published that same year. It does not seem to have attracted special attention, and during the thirty years following it is not found in many hymn books. But such postponement is a commonplace in the history of hymns. The turn of this hymn came early in the nineteenth century, and it gradually advanced to the first place as regards the proportion of church hymnals that found room for it.

SOME POINTS FOR DISCUSSION

1. The Scriptures from which the imagery is taken, in the passage of the Wesleys' *Hymns on the Lord's Supper* and in the first verse of Toplady's hymn, seem to be the cleft rock of Ex. 33:22 and the smitten rock of Ex. 17:6, and these as interpreted by I Cor. 10:4, " And that Rock was Christ," and by the pierced side of Jesus, with the outflow of water and blood. Dr. Oliver Wendell Holmes said it was these material images that made the hymn so impressive. Are the images confused in the hymn? The Rev. William Henry Havergal thought so, and tried to make two hymns of it; one on the Rock as the Shelter, the other on the Rock as the Source of the water of life. But no one seemed to care for his hymns.

The beautiful phrase, " Rock of Ages," is also Scriptural. Toplady took it from the reading, in the margin of the King James Version, of Isa. 26:4.

2. In printing the hymn in his *Psalms and Hymns*, Toplady made some changes in it. The one for which we are most grateful is in the new title of the hymn, which leaves Mr. Wesley out. It reads " A Prayer, living and dying." He now began the fourth verse with " while " in place of the hissing " whilst." And he put " When I soar to worlds unknown " for " When I soar through tracts unknown." Is this change an improvement?

The Hymnal revised follows this text, except in reading " When my eylids close in death " in place of " When my eye-strings break in death." It was a mistaken notion that in dying the muscles or tendons of the eye snapped. Shakespeare uses the same phrase in his *Cymbeline*. The new line has been substituted by general consent. As actual fact is in question, would not " When mine eyes are closed in death " be still nearer the truth?

In 1815 the Rev. Thomas Cotterill of Sheffield condensed the four verses into three for a hymn book of his own. For many years this three-verse form of the hymn was the only one known in Episcopalian and Methodist hymn books. But the full form of the hymn has now prevailed.

3. Of the *tunes* for this hymn in *The Hymnal revised*, that by Redhead, to which he gave no name, is most popular in England. It was Number 76 in his book of *Church Hymn Tunes*, 1853, and is generally known as " Redhead Number 76." In this country Thomas Hastings' " Toplady " is more popular. He wrote it for a hymn book called *Spiritual Songs* that came out as a series of little pamphlets, beginning in 1830, and was designed to combat the introduction of revival and ballad tunes into Presbyterian churches by offering some that were more reverent and yet simple and easy to sing. The tune " Reliance," Number 322 in *The Hymnal revised*, was also composed for this hymn at the request of the committee in charge of the original edition. In revising the book it was thought best to set other words to this tune. Its composer was an English musician, then living in Denver.

XI

GOD OF OUR FATHERS, WHOSE ALMIGHTY HAND

THE TEXT OF THE HYMN

1 God of our fathers, whose almighty hand
Leads forth in beauty all the starry band
Of shining worlds in splendor through the skies,
Our grateful songs before Thy throne arise.

2 Thy love Divine hath led us in the past;
In this free land by Thee our lot is cast;
Be Thou our Ruler, Guardian, Guide, and Stay;
Thy word our law, Thy paths our chosen way.

3 From war's alarms, from deadly pestilence,
Be Thy strong arm our ever sure defence;
Thy true religion in our hearts increase,
Thy bounteous goodness nourish us in peace.

4 Refresh Thy people on their toilsome way,
Lead us from night to never-ending day;
Fill all our lives with love and grace Divine,
And glory, laud, and praise be ever Thine.

Rev. Daniel C. Roberts, 1876

NOTE: The text is that printed in the Report of the Protestant Episcopal Hymnal Commission to the General Convention of 1892.

This Fourth of July hymn was written in 1876 by Dr. Daniel C. Roberts, a New England clergyman, for the centennial of the Declaration of Independence. It seems at first a far cry from this hymn to those of the eighteenth century revival in old England which we have been studying together; but there is, after all, a real connection between the political events the new hymn celebrates and the great revival out of which the old ones came.

The fact is that in England, as the fourth day of July, 1776, approached, most of the people were a great deal more excited about the prospect of war with the American colonies than about the progress of the revival; and none more concerned than were the leaders of the revival, which had made new bonds between the old country and the colonies. Whitefield had gone over to them again and again with his flaming gospel, and in one of them his worn-out body had lain at rest since 1770; but a host of his American converts remained. Both of the Wesleys also had lived in the colonies, and the American Methodists now numbered some thousands.

John Wesley's sympathies were with the Americans at first. Then his sense of loyalty changed his mind, and he printed *A calm Address to our American Colonies.* In this he appropriated, with or without permission, the contents of a pamphlet, *Taxation no tyranny*, by that same Dr. Johnson who gave a coin to the girl with a hymn book in her hand. It was then that the redoubtable Mr. Toplady put forth his *An old Fox tarr'd and feather'd.* Toplady was earnestly opposed to making war against the Americans, but it was not in their behalf that he published his pamphlet. His intention, as he said, was, first, to show Wesley's dishonesty in stealing Dr. Johnson's materials, " and, second, to raise a little skin by giving the Fox a gentle flogging as a turn-coat." That was in October, 1775. A few months later Mr. Toplady

printed something pleasanter to remember — his " Rock
of Ages, cleft for me." That was in March, 1776. It is,
of course, nothing more than an interesting coincidence
that the centennial year of the Declaration of Independence in which Dr. Roberts' hymn was written was also
the centennial year of " Rock of Ages." And in view of
its great influence in both England and America, Toplady's hymn might well have had a little centennial celebration all its own.

A CENTENNIAL HYMN

When the present writer was gathering materials for
The Hymnal, published in 1895, he became familiar with
the hymn " God of our fathers," by the Rev. Daniel C.
Roberts, set to George William Warren's music in that
musical edition of the Protestant Episcopal Hymnal
of 1892, commonly called " Tucker's Hymnal." Mr.
Warren was a warm personal friend. Dr. Roberts
showed himself friendly. Permission to use hymn and
tune was readily given. And so the hymn got into *The
Hymnal*.

An unfamiliar hymn in a church hymnal is always a
venture, especially one with long lines. Would this one
" take "? It soon became plain that it was being used
in patriotic services; and at the end of 1900 the present
writer, having in mind a study such as this, so long de-
ferred, asked the author for some account of the hymn
and for a copy of it by his own hand.

Dr. Roberts very kindly furnished the requested autograph, which is here reproduced in facsimile; and this
is what he wrote from Concord, New Hampshire, on
January 8, 1901:

" The hymn was written in 1876 for a celebration of the Centennial ' Fourth ' of July, and sung at Brandon, Vermont, to the tune called ' Russian Hymn,' set to ' Rise, crowned with light ' in our Hymnals. When our General Convention appointed a Commission to revise the Hymnal, I sent it, without my name, promising to send the name if the hymn were accepted. It was accepted, and printed anonymously in the report of the Commission. Before the Hymnal was printed, the Rev[d] Dr. Tucker, late of Troy, editor of our best musical Hymnal, and Mr. Geo. Wm. Warren, organist of S. Thomas' Church, New York, were appointed a committee to choose a hymn for the centennial celebration of the adoption of the Constitution. They selected this hymn, then anonymous, and, wanting a tune, Mr. Warren composed a tune to which it has since been set in the ' Tucker ' Hymnal. Subsequently it was selected as the ' Recessional ' at the ' Bi-Centenary ' of Trinity Church, New York City.

" My little hymn has thus had very flattering official recognition. But that which would really gladden my heart, popular recognition, it has not received. Mr. Warren's tune is majestic. Mr. Parker's in Hutchins' Hymnal rather academic: the kind of tune appealing to the ' Demos ' has not appeared. I should be more than gratified if the ' people ' should take it up. In fact, I confess, that after its favorable official reception, I had a little hope which took the form of an ambition, that it might be so. But that has not happened. Recognition from you is very grateful to me. It had never occurred to me to think of it as of value, until the incidents above related befell, and then I allowed myself to dream a little."

God of our fathers, whose almighty hand
Leads forth in beauty all the starry band
Of shining worlds in splendor through
   the skies,
Our grateful songs before thy throne
   arise.

Thy love divine hath led us in the
   past;
In this free land by Thee our lot
   is cast;
Be Thou our Ruler, Guardian, Guide
   and stay,
Thy Word our law, Thy paths our
   chosen way.

From war's alarms, from deadly
   pestilence,
Be Thy strong arm our ever sure
   defence;
Thy true religion in our hearts
   increase,
Thy bounteous goodness nourish
   us in peace.

Refresh Thy people on their toilsome
   way,
Lead us from night to never ending
   day;
Fill all our lives with love and
   grace divine,
And glory, laud and praise be
   ever thine.

Dan'l C. Roberts

MR. WARREN'S "NATIONAL HYMN"

Dr. Roberts' letter, with its frank human touch, is very engaging, but he did not understand how heavy the odds are against any new hymn getting a real hearing, even after it has edged its way into our over-full church hymnals. If he were now alive he would see that this hymn has won its present favor very largely through the appeal of the music Mr. Warren composed for it. And that makes it proper that we should also give Mr. Warren his share of the credit.

George William Warren was born in the city of Albany in 1828 and was educated at Racine College. Although he became Professor of Music at Columbia University, his musical education was due to his own indefatigable efforts: he was self-taught. Early in life he composed a number of piano pieces, and the royalties from one of them, "Tam o' Shanter," brought him quite a little income every year to the end of his life. He was an organist and choirmaster from the age of eighteen, at Albany, Brooklyn, and for more than thirty years at St. Thomas' in New York. These were the years of his greatest power and reputation; and the music of St. Thomas' became a popular feature of New York life, drawing crowds to the church. His tunes, mostly composed for St. Thomas' choir, belonged rather to the older parlor-music school than to the later "Anglican" school. They were spontaneous and melodious, and were full of feeling, as the composer himself was.

He was a man of high-strung temperament, of deep affections, a sincere manner, and rather blunt speech. He died of apoplexy on March 17, 1902, and was buried from the church he loved with a solemn service in which

there was not a note of music, even of the organ. It was
intended to suggest that there was no one any longer to
lead the music of St. Thomas'; and it was in contrast
with an earlier commemoration of Mr. Warren's twenty-
five years of service, at which all the music was of his
composition and his tune to Dr. Roberts' hymn was sung
as the processional.

Mr. Warren contributed two tunes to *The Hymnal* of
1895, one of which, " Log College," is retained in *The
Hymnal revised.* It was quite characteristic of him that
he refused to receive any compensation for this tune,
preferring that it should appear as a mark of friendship
for the writer of the words and the editor of the book.

THE AUTHOR OF THE CENTENNIAL HYMN

Dr. Roberts' letter of 1901 went on to say:

" My personal history is of little account. I was born
in Bridge Hampton, Long Island, N. Y., Nov. 5th 1841.
Entered Kenyon College, Gambier, Ohio, in 1857. Enlisted as a private in 1862. Was ordained Deacon in
1865, Priest in 1866. Served as Rector of Christ Church,
Montpelier, Vermont; S. John's, Lowell, Mass.; S.
Thomas's, Brandon, Vermont, and for the last twenty-
three years have been Vicar of S. Paul's Church, Concord, N. H., of which parish the Bishop of New Hampshire is titular Rector. I remain a country Parson,
known only within my own small world."

This is the brief life record of a man efficient in his
parishes and trusted in the wider councils of his denomination. He had more recognition than he has admitted:
as a Mason and a Civil War veteran; as President of
the State Historical Society while in New Hampshire,

and President of the State Normal School in Vermont. He was apparently a good, manly, warm-hearted, clear-headed, hard-working clergyman: one of a type of which no Church can have too many examples. Some occasional verses and carols reveal another turn of his mind and hand. He would have been the last to claim that they revealed him as a poet. Dr. Roberts died " on the Vigil of All Saints Day " of 1907: so the denominational newspapers reported. Some of their readers might have preferred a simpler record of the date.

The regiment in which Dr. Roberts enlisted in 1862 was the Eighty-fourth Regiment of Ohio Volunteers. Like so many of those who survived the great adventure of the Civil War, he was always afterward at heart a veteran soldier. Indeed he reëntered military service as chaplain in the National Guard of New Hampshire. It may therefore be fitting that this brief record of his life should close with the last verse of his own word picture of a soldier's day, which he printed as *War Etchings:*

> Now silence broods with shadowy wings,
> The watchful sentry's footfall rings,
> The soldier sleeps beneath the sky,
> While night winds murmur lullaby.

SOME POINTS FOR DISCUSSION

1. When we attain the perfection to which Mr. Wesley summoned us, to the great indignation of Mr. Toplady, we shall no doubt be able to write perfect hymns. Dr. Roberts had not yet attained perfection in the art of writing verse, and his hymn is not free from faults.

That it begins with the same phrase as Kipling's " Recessional " does, is a bit unfortunate, but no fault of

DR. DANIEL C. ROBERTS

Dr. Roberts, since Kipling's fine hymn was yet unwritten. It is, however, a question whether the opening lines, with their majestic figure of the Almighty leading forth the processional of starry worlds, are quite lived up to in the lines that follow. It may be interesting to compare the hymn in this respect with Mr. Chadwick's " Eternal Ruler of the ceaseless round " (No. 351 in *The Hymnal revised*), which opens with the same figure. And then, if we are to sing a number of verses to the same tune, it is plain that the accents or stresses of the voice should be distributed uniformly, so that the emphasis in the music and in the words should match throughout. Do any of these lines fail in that respect, and, if so, which lines?

The hymn is a metrical prayer, not very poetical and hardly more eloquent than many an extemporized prayer one might hear from the pulpit on patriotic occasions. But it is devout and dignified and serviceable. It has the heart of the matter in it. Mr. Warren's trumpets call to the congregation, and the people respond gladly, and not without a thrill " for God and country." Perhaps we can hardly think of the hymn apart from Mr. Warren's music. But then we do not have to.

2. Of all the hymns written for the centennial of American independence, this is the only one that appears to have found a permanent place in our hymn books. Attempts have been made to get a hearing for Whittier's " Centennial Hymn," beginning,

> Our fathers' God! from out whose hand
> The centuries fall like grains of sand.

But his verses are so true to the particular occasion for which they were written that they are not easily adapted to a more general use.

3. The great World War made unexpected demands upon our limited stock of patriotic songs. And it may be a question still whether we have a full supply of good hymns for the Fourth of July. If more are needed, it might be worthwhile for anyone who has a copy of the old *Presbyterian Hymnal* of 1874 to take a look at the " Hymn for the Fourth of July, 1832," by the author of " The Star-Spangled Banner," which begins,

> Before the Lord we bow —
> The God who reigns above,
> And rules the world below,
> Boundless in power and love.

Meantime it is satisfactory to have Dr. Roberts' hymn to commemorate the Centennial, alongside of Dr. Bacon's " O God, beneath Thy guiding hand," commemorating the Pilgrim Fathers, and Dr. Holmes' " O Lord of hosts, Almighty King! " commemorating the Civil War.

XII

HOW SWEET THE NAME OF JESUS SOUNDS

THE TEXT OF THE HYMN

1 How sweet the Name of Jesus sounds
   In a believer's ear!
   It soothes his sorrows, heals his wounds,
   And drives away his fear.

2 It makes the wounded spirit whole,
   And calms the troubled breast;
   'Tis Manna to the hungry soul,
   And to the weary Rest.

3 Dear Name! the Rock on which I build,
   My Shield and Hiding-place,
   My never-failing Treasury, filled
   With boundless stores of grace;

4 Jesus, my Shepherd, Brother, Friend,
   My Prophet, Priest, and King,
   My Lord, my Life, my Way, my End,
   Accept the praise I bring.

5 Weak is the effort of my heart,
   And cold my warmest thought;
   But when I see Thee as Thou art,
   I'll praise Thee as I ought.

6 Till then I would Thy love proclaim
   With every fleeting breath;
   And may the music of Thy Name
   Refresh my soul in death.

Rev. John Newton, 1779

NOTE: The text is taken from the first edition of Newton's *Olney Hymns*, 1779, with the omission of the original fourth verse and the change of "Husband" to "Brother" in the fourth verse as here numbered.

When "good Lady Huntingdon" seceded from the Church of England, a number of the clergy who had helped her work felt it their duty to remain in the old Church, although they knew very well that they were not wanted. They formed themselves into that Evangelical, or, as we usually call it, Low Church Party of which we heard in connection with Mr. Toplady. These men were Calvinistic in their theology, and claimed their right to preach the gospel as they believed it, and also to sing evangelical hymns in church as well as the metrical Psalms bound up with the prayer books. With not much of a party organization, these Evangelicals tried to carry on the revival, in London when they could, but mostly in the isolation of their country parishes.

"OLNEY HYMNS"

The story of the hymn whose title heads this chapter takes us into one of those country parishes, Olney, on the bank of the river Ouse, in the county of Buckinghamshire. The little town consisted mostly, and does yet, of one street, widening into a market place; the most conspicuous object being the parish church, with its ungraceful spire. The town was not pretty, nor the people well-to-do or well educated. Many pilgrims go to Olney nowadays for the poet Cowper's sake. But what first carried its name far and wide in England and America was nothing other than a hymn book written there and called *Olney Hymns*.

The pulpit of the parish church was filled by a bluff and manly Evangelical, John Newton, whose looks and ways brought a whiff of the sea. He had been a sailor, and in 1764 was ordained and appointed a curate of the parish, the vicar being of the absentee sort.

JOHN NEWTON

Newton's preaching began to fill the church, but he gave special attention to young people's work and secured permission to use Lord Dartmouth's empty mansion, the Great House. Here of a Thursday afternoon he gathered the children, not for the usual catechism exercise, but to explain the Scriptures " in their own little way." In the evenings he had meetings for older people, with extempore prayers and exhortation; and he introduced the singing of hymns. All of which may seem commonplace now; but it was quite enough then and there to stamp the curate a " Methodist," as the hard-and-fast Churchman dubbed all Evangelicals. And one at least of Newton's neighboring rectors refused to speak to him when they passed.

It was for these revival meetings at the Great House that Newton began to write hymns of his own, not venturing as yet to displace the metrical Psalms from the parish church services. And that is the reason most of his hymns are so confined to personal spiritual experiences. They have the anxious tone that a pastor's preaching takes in time of revival. He wrote only one great song of praise, the still familiar " Glorious things of thee are spoken."

Newton was not a poet and did not pretend to be one. " There is," he said, " a stile and manner suited to the composition of hymns, which may be more successfully, or at least more easily attained by a versifier, than by a poet." He was writing for plain people, and made his hymns so simple that these could follow and understand. In all this he took his cue from Dr. Watts. Newton had a ready pen, some imagination, deep feeling, a knowledge of Scripture, and an urgent motive; something else, also, that we may best call the power of virility. And once

in a while, as in this hymn and in " Quiet, Lord, my fro-
ward heart," he climbed nearer to the heights where poets
walk.

At one time Newton was writing a hymn every week
for his prayer meeting, where no doubt they were given
out verse by verse or even by couplets. By 1779 they
mounted up to two hundred and eighty, and that year he
gathered them with sixty-eight more by his friend and
neighbor, William Cowper, and published them at
London as

OLNEY HYMNS,

IN

THREE BOOKS.

> Book I. On select Texts of SCRIPTURE.
>
> Book II. On occasional SUBJECTS.
>
> Book III. On the Progress and Changes
>   of the SPIRITUAL LIFE.

None of the hymns is dated. " How sweet the Name of
Jesus sounds " is No. 57 of " Book I. On select Texts of
Scripture." Its text is Solomon's Song, chapter 1 :3 ; and
its title is " The name of JESUS."

Olney Hymns is best understood as a revival hymn
book. In its day it had the same welcome and popularity
that *Gospel Hymns* of the Moody and Sankey revival had
in ours. But the books cannot be compared, since it was
the music of *Gospel Hymns* that won the day. *Olney
Hymns* had no tunes at all, but its hymns exactly met
the need of the Evangelical preachers and their converts.
It was the Evangelical theology put into rhyme for singing, but even more for reading and remembering. It
became an Evangelical handbook, printed over and over
in England and America, and it exerted an immense in-

fluence. The simple verses exercised over many minds
the fascination that nursery rhymes have for children.
The Roman Catholic hymn writer, Faber, speaks of their
acting like a spell upon him for many years in his Protestant youth and coming back unbidden through his
Catholic years. And now that the career of *Olney Hymns*
is run, a few of its choicer strains survive among the
permanent treasures of the Church.

JOHN NEWTON'S ROMANTIC CAREER

The curate of Olney was a marked man; not only because he was an Evangelical, but because he was " a man
with a past." He was one of those whom people point
to in the street with a nudge and a " Do you know about
him? " This was due to the startling disclosure of his
experiences he published just after coming to Olney as
" The authentic Narrative " of his life. It was a record
of debauchery, and it would be hard for one man to
paint an enemy as black as Newton painted himself
in that book.

He was born in London in July, 1725, of a godly
mother who lived long enough to make a religious impression upon his childish heart. His father was captain
of a merchantman in the Mediterranean trade; a severe,
silent man, of whom the boy was rather afraid. At the
age of eleven he was taken from school, and went to sea
with his father on half a dozen voyages. The boy plainly
was hot-blooded, willful, and " irregular " in his conduct.
But he was far from passing these years without
" troublesome convictions " and religious experiences.
" I think I took up and laid aside a religious profession
three or four times before I was sixteen years of age; but

all this while my heart was insincere. I often saw a necessity of religion as a means of escaping hell; but I loved sin, and was unwilling to forsake it." His " last reform " was the most remarkable; a year or more of prayer and Scripture-reading covering " the greatest part of every day." As far as shipboard conditions would permit, he became an ascetic, avoiding conversation, eating no meat, and " bemoaning his former miscarriages."

It may all have been mistaken, but it does not sound " insincere," as Newton called it. Surely to persevere in such a course in face of a jeering crew and of the temptations of southern ports shows a certain strength of character. It left Newton dull and disheartened, and an easy victim to some skeptical literature that fell in his way. Before long he had lost all sense of religious reality. He became an utter skeptic, " an infidel," as he said; and with " the way prepared for all that is to follow."

Returning from a voyage to Venice in 1743, he was impressed on board a warship, but through his father's influence rated a midshipman. He deserted, was caught, brought back to Plymouth in chains, publicly flogged, and degraded to the rank of a common seaman. His disgrace, which he thought undeserved, embittered and hardened him. Quite reckless now, he plunged, according to his own testimony, into a career of degrading debauchery and moral shamelessness, and, " like one infected with a pestilence, was capable of spreading a taint wherever I went."

He effected an exchange from the warship, glad to be rid of him, into a slave ship bound for the coast of Africa: his thought being that there he could " be as abandoned as I pleased, without any control." He entered the service of a slave trader in one of the Plantane Islands, was treated with abominable cruelty and neglect, and went down into a depth of physical degradation where even most of the Negro slaves refused any dealings with him.

In the end he got word to his father, and was rescued by a vessel commissioned to look out for him. On the way home he encountered a violent storm and was almost lost. In the stress a review of his past life brought him to shame, and from shame to prayer. He started out deliberately to rediscover the grounds of faith in the Gospels he had become accustomed to laugh over; and step by step he went forward toward the reality and assurance of faith. He reached England in May, 1748, a Christian by conviction, though still feeling his way.

Through all these wander-years Newton carried two talismans, a boy's memory of his mother and a man's love for a young girl he had left behind him in England. On his return the girl married him — with a heroic trust, one would think. In seeking a livelihood Newton's new convictions did not prevent his entering the slave trade. The moral standards of the time had not yet condemned it. He made two voyages to Africa and the West Indies, and only an attack of apoplexy prevented a third.

He was appointed tide surveyor at Liverpool in 1755, and held the post several years. There he came under the direct influence of Whitefield and the Evangelical Revival. He carried on his studies (even at his lowest he had never wholly foregone them), began to preach occasionally as a lay evangelist, and felt the call to enter the ministry. He wavered between the established and dissenting churches, and chose the established. But he could not find in all England a bishop willing to ordain him, until Lord Dartmouth came to his rescue. Dartmouth was Secretary of State in charge of America, friendly to the colonies, and after him our Dartmouth College was named. He was at the same time an Evangelical and a liberal helper of Lady Huntingdon. He made new interest in high quarters and secured Newton's ordination on agreeing to appoint him to the curacy of Olney. Newton " was too much in earnest about religion to be readily entrusted with a commission to teach it,

By these truths, the Lord is please   p hold me. My trial is very g but He has said, My Grace is sufficient for thee. So I humbly ho to find it.   Give my cordial love to dear Mrs West. May the L bless you both, and make you blessings to each other, and to Me Amen!

I am, Dear Mad am,

Your affectionate o

N: 6.   *19 June 1801*   *John Ne*

A PASSAGE FROM AN AUTOGRAPH LETTER

except as a matter of favour to a great man: " — so Sir George Otto Trevelyan remarks in his delightful book, *The American Revolution.* It is possible also that Newton's record seemed very " irregular " to the bishops.

In his own heart that record was indelible. He became a faithful pastor, at Olney for nearly sixteen years, and at St. Mary Woolnoth, London, for twenty-eight more.* He became a leader of the Evangelical Party, loved and trusted. But in his own heart, and on his own

* " My race at Olney is nearly finished; I am about to form a connection for life with one Mary Woolnoth, a respected London saint in Lombard Street." (Newton to Bull, Sept. 21, 1779.)

tongue, to the end of his life, he was always " the old African blasphemer." Was he really called upon, we sometimes ask, to publish that Narrative and continually to blacken a good name fairly won? He thought so. He was the living proof that God could save even to the uttermost. And he thought he was called upon to give his testimony in plain terms and at any cost.

Into his hymns also Newton's experiences are written deep. One day, when his memory was almost gone, he said, " I can never forget two things: first, that I was a great sinner, and, second, that Jesus is a great Saviour." The first memory explains an undertone of sadness in the hymns: the second explains why he wrote " How sweet the Name of Jesus sounds."

Newton lived to be eighty-two, and died December 21, 1807. He was buried beneath his church of St. Mary Woolnoth, and a tablet was placed on the church wall with a touching inscription prepared by himself: —

JOHN NEWTON
CLERK,
ONCE AN INFIDEL AND LIBERTINE,
A SERVANT OF SLAVES IN AFRICA,
WAS,
BY THE RICH MERCY OF OUR LORD AND SAVIOUR
JESUS CHRIST,

PRESERVED, RESTORED, PARDONED,
AND APPOINTED TO PREACH THE FAITH
HE HAD LONG LABOURED TO DESTROY.

HE MINISTERED
NEAR XVI. YEARS AS CURATE AND VICAR
OF OLNEY IN BUCKS,
AND XXVIII. AS RECTOR
OF THESE UNITED PARISHES.

In 1893 the excavations for the London underground railway disturbed the church vaults; and Newton's remains were removed and reburied in the churchyard at Olney.

SOME POINTS FOR DISCUSSION

1. The Daily Service book of the Roman Catholic Church has an office for the " Feast of the Most Holy Name of Jesus." It includes two parts of one of the most beautiful of Latin hymns, " Jesu, dulcis memoria." The Rev. Samuel W. Duffield, a Presbyterian lover of Latin hymns, thought it probable that these verses of Newton on the Name of Jesus are " an echo or paraphrase " of the Latin original. One wishes he had said why he thought so. Eighteenth century Evangelicals were not much interested in Latin hymns. But in this matter we have the materials at hand on which to base our own conclusion. Good translations of both parts of the Latin hymn are in *The Hymnal revised:* " Jesus, the very thought of Thee " (No. 545) and " O Jesus, King most wonderful " (No. 144). Is there any similarity between these and Newton's hymn?

2. As originally written, " How sweet the Name of Jesus sounds " had seven verses. The weakest of these is omitted from *The Hymnal revised;* the original fourth verse. It ran,

> " By thee my pray'rs acceptance gain,
>   Altho' with sin defil'd:
> Satan accuses me in vain,
>   And I am own'd a child."

Is the hymn better without this verse, or should it be restored?

3. There is also a change of one word from the original text of the first line of the present fourth verse, which read,

"Jesus! My Shepherd, Husband, Friend."

We all dislike such changes from what an author wrote. But if men are to go to church at all, how can they address Christ as their husband? Was it not the Church rather than the individual Christian that was described as the Bride of Christ?

4. In singing the first verse we have to pronounce "wounds" in such a way that the rhyme with "sounds" may be preserved. It is no great hardship, as Shakspeare, Marlowe, and Pope did the same thing habitually. In other connections it may be best to conform to recent usage by pronouncing the word as woond.

XIII

GOD MOVES IN A MYSTERIOUS WAY

THE TEXT OF THE HYMN

1 God moves in a mysterious way
  His wonders to perform;
  He plants His footsteps in the sea,
  And rides upon the storm.

2 Deep in unfathomable mines
  Of never-failing skill
  He treasures up His bright designs,
  And works His sovereign will.

3 Ye fearful saints, fresh courage take;
  The clouds ye so much dread
  Are big with mercy, and shall break
  In blessings on your head.

4 Judge not the Lord by feeble sense,
  But trust Him for His grace;
  Behind a frowning providence
  He hides a smiling face.

5 His purposes will ripen fast,
  Unfolding every hour;
  The bud may have a bitter taste,
  But sweet will be the flower.

6 Blind unbelief is sure to err,
  And scan His work in vain;
  God is His own Interpreter,
  And He will make it plain.

William Cowper, 1774

NOTE: The text is taken from John Newton's *Twenty-six Letters on religious subjects*, London, 1774: from which book the hymn passed into *Olney Hymns* of 1779 without change.

The names of John Newton, curate of Olney, and his neighbor, William Cowper, poet and author of this hymn, join together as naturally as if they were partners in a firm of " Newton and Cowper." Their lives were knit in one of the historic friendships. And they were indeed literary partners as joint authors of *Olney Hymns,* the famous hymn book of the Evangelical Party in the Church of England. Newton was the senior partner, and it was only after the dissolution of the firm that the junior partner became famous.

HOW THE POET CAME TO OLNEY

William Cowper (he pronounced it Cooper) was born in the rectory of Berkhampstead in November, 1731. Left motherless when only six, he was sent to boarding school, and never forgot what he endured there from a big bully. He was taken away on account of eye trouble, and at the age of ten placed in the Westminster School at London. He said afterwards that he left school as ignorant of religion as the satchel at his back, but in that he was very like many other boys. He was articled to an attorney in whose office he idled away " three misspent years." At the age of twenty-one he entered the Temple as a regular student of law; not because he had any drawing to that profession, but to please his father. He came of a legal family, his father being brother of a judge and nephew of a lord chancellor. He was admitted to the bar in 1754.

The young lawyer made no attempt to practice. He made his office a gathering place of young wits. He kept up his classics, began to write verse, and sought gayety. He fell in love, first with his cousin Theodora, whose father interposed, and again with a girl of Greenwich; but his ardor cooled. If his life seems idle, it was perhaps busy in trying to forget himself. For he was already in the grip of the saddest of human ailments, brain disease. As soon as he began to live alone in the Temple, it showed itself. Gradually he lapsed into dreadful depression. " Day and night I was upon the rack, lying down in horror and rising up in despair."

After a year of it he taught himself to pray, and composed a little liturgy. On recovering his spirits he threw the liturgy into the fire and relapsed into careless ways. Meantime he was using up the little money he had. His prospects at the bar were so hopeless that in his thirty-second year a relative got him an appointment to a clerkship in the House of Lords. Some difficulties arose, and the dread of having to stand a public examination so wrought upon him that he lost his reason and made several attempts to kill himself.

These left behind an unutterable anguish and the firm conviction that he was sentenced already to eternal damnation; as he wrote,

> Damned below Judas; more abhorred than he was,
> Who for a few pence sold his holy Master:

and so through those dreadful lines in which he envies the fate of the dead consigned to perdition, while he, fed with judgment, is buried above ground in a fleshly tomb. Visions and voices haunted him; an awful darkness fell; heavy blows of some great hammer beat upon the brain; body and soul writhed in pain. Cowper was insane. There was nothing to do but to send him to an asylum at St. Albans.

After eight months of despair the light began to glim-

Drawn by W. Harvey from an Original by Romney.   Engraved by J. Stow.

believe me yours

Wm Cowper.

mer during a visit of his brother. Deliriums and delusions weakened, and he caught glimpses of God's mercy. Opening the Bible at Rom. 3:25 one day, " Immediately I received strength to believe, and the full beams of the Sun of Righteousness shone upon me." In that inward radiance he was content to spend a year of convalescence at St. Albans.

When Cowper left the asylum and took the lodgings at Huntingdon his brother had provided, he needed surely the inward comfort of his new evangelical faith. For outward things were pretty forlorn. He was thirty-three; he had failed in his profession, was dependent upon his relatives, was separated from all his friendships, and was, to put it gently, an invalid. Happily he found new friends in the Rev. Mr. Unwin and his family. They agreed to take Cowper into their cheerful home, where he lived contentedly with them until Mr. Unwin's sudden death in 1767. It is interesting to note in passing Cowper's references to the family custom of gathering to sing out of the new hymn book of the Rev. Martin Madan, one of the Evangelical leaders; because they show one of the ways in which the new Evangelical hymns were insinuating themselves into Church of England households to supplement the metrical Psalms they were expected to use at church.

After Unwin's death there happened one of those seemingly casual incidents that change the course of men's lives. It was nothing more than a call of condolence from the Rev. John Newton, curate of Olney. Cowper had made up his mind to continue living with Mrs. Unwin, " whose behavior to me has been that of a mother to a son." And now both were so much drawn to Newton that they decided to move to Olney for the sake of

being under his ministry. At their request he engaged
for them a house in the market place of that town, then
called " Orchard Side " and now kept up as the Cowper
and Newton Museum.

THE POET'S SHARE IN " OLNEY HYMNS "

Only an orchard lay between the gardens of Newton's
vicarage and the house he chose for Cowper. They made
an opening in the vicarage wall; they wore a path across
the orchard, and they joined their hearts and lives in

THE COWPER AND NEWTON MUSEUM, OLNEY

an inseparable friendship. Newton thoroughly appreciated Cowper, loved him tenderly, and no doubt in his
own way tried to protect that sensitive nature against
its own infirmity. Naturally he saw the importance of
keeping Cowper's mind occupied, but he would not have
been the fervent Evangelical he was if he had not made
his friend's gift contribute to the work that absorbed his
own energies. He engaged Cowper in visiting the sick
and dying, persuaded him to lead the extempore prayers
at the evening meetings, and to write hymns to be sung

there after the sermon. It was for the occasion of re-
moving those meetings to the larger room of the Great
House that Cowper furnished his "Jesus, where'er Thy
people meet."

Other hymns express plainly Cowper's own experiences; now cheerful, as in "Sometimes a Light sur-
prises"; now retrospective, as he recalls that sudden
radiance upon the text in Romans,

> The Spirit breathes upon the word,
> And brings the truth to sight;

now regretful of the fading of the joyfulness of those
latter days at St. Albans,

> Where is the blessedness I knew
> When first I saw the Lord?

and now in the depths of despondency,

> My former hopes are dead,
> My terror now begins;
> I feel, alas! that I am dead
> In trespasses and sins.

For again the shadows were closing in. It may be that
the revival atmosphere at Olney was too highly charged
for Cowper. It may be that Newton was unwise in
asking for those agitating public appearances at the
Great House. It may be merely that Cowper's disease
was approaching an inevitable outbreak. Whatever the
occasion may have been, the visions and voices came
back; black melancholy settled down. The voices told
Cowper that God demanded his life in sacrifice, and once
more he attempted suicide.

With that catastrophe the hymn we are now studying
is closely connected. It was the last, and has been gen-

erally regarded as the outcome of the attempt at suicide. That was in October, 1773. Since *The Hymnal* was first printed, some new evidence as to its date has come to light. The writer is at present disposed to think it was written toward the end of 1772 or very early in 1773. This date gives added probability to the substantial accuracy of the statement in the Rev. Samuel Greatheed's funeral sermon that Cowper " conceived some presentiment " of the attack of insanity, and that " as it drew near, during a solitary walk in the fields," he composed this hymn " so expressive of that faith and hope which he attained so long as he possessed himself." Newton testifies that even in the midst of his distress and foreboding, and up to the date of the " terrible dream " that broke his heart early in 1773, Cowper often expressed his submission to God's sovereignty, and said that God was trying him only for the purpose of bringing about some good thing.

Cowper's attack put an end to his hymn-writing. And it is only with Cowper the hymn writer we have here to deal. He was to recover from this attack and to spend years of comparative peace of mind and of poetic achievement before the last onset of insanity ending only with his death in 1800. Cowper was over fifty years of age when he published his first volume of poems, and one likes to think of the fame he won as some compensation for the sorrows he endured. It was perhaps out of his sorrows he wrought that tender grace of his verse which keeps it still alive when the work of his contemporary poets lies so dead and forgotten. In all his serious poetry Cowper aimed to be the " poet of Christianity." And it was the Christianity of the Evangelical Revival; Christianity as accepted and taught by the Evangelical Party in the Church of England. His poems have indeed (quite recently) been described as " Methodism in verse."

Cowper's hymns, with very few exceptions, were first put into print by John Newton. This particular one he printed in his *Twenty-six Letters on religious subjects* in 1774. It was copied into *The Gospel Magazine* for July of the same year. In that year also it began its career in the hymn books, being included in the " Collection " of the Rev. Mr. Conyers, another of the Evangelical Party. Its place in the affections of the Church it has never lost.

The hymn appeared again in *Olney Hymns* of 1779, with all the others Cowper had written before the attack of 1773. Newton explains the situation in a preface. It is odd that so many readers of books always skip the preface, generally the most human part of a book. Newton's is quite touching. " The whole number [of hymns] were composed by two persons only. The original design would not admit of any other association." The book " was intended as a monument, to perpetuate the remembrance of an intimate and endeared friendship. With this pleasing view I entered upon my part, which would have been much smaller than it is, and the book would have appeared much sooner, and in a very different form, if the wise, though mysterious providence of God, had not seen fit to cross my wishes. We had not proceeded far upon our proposed plan, before my dear friend was prevented, by a long and affecting indisposition, from affording me any further assistance. My grief and disappointment were great; I hung my harp upon the willows, and for some time thought myself determined to proceed no further without him. Yet my mind was afterwards led to assume the service. My progress in it, amidst a variety of other engagements, has been slow, yet in a course of years the hymns amounted to a considerable number. And my deference to the judgment and desires of others, has at length overcome the reluctance I long felt to see them in print, while I had so few of my friend's hymns to insert in the collection."

SOME POINTS FOR DISCUSSION

1. When the earlier series of these studies was gathered into a book, a reviewer of it began by saying, " No great poet has ever written a hymn." His remark suggests several interesting topics for discussion. (1) Is there any more ground for expecting a great poet to write a hymn, simply because poems and hymns are both in verse, than there is for expecting a great novelist to write a sermon, simply because novels and sermons are both in prose? (2) Is it not probable that most great poets would be glad to write a great hymn? Poets like recognition and crave immortality. Is not the vision of multitudes singing their words for years and perhaps for centuries likely to appeal to them? (3) Are all great poets able to write great hymns? Some of them cannot even write a good song. But to write a good hymn requires much more than a lyrical gift. When Dr. Jowett appealed to Lord Tennyson to write " a few hymns in a high strain," that great poet replied by saying that " to write a good hymn was the most difficult thing in the world." (4) But when all is said, some great and many eminent poets have in fact written hymns. Among English poets the names of Ben Jonson, Milton, Wordsworth, Scott, Tennyson, and Kipling, come to mind at once; and on this side of the water those of Emerson, Longfellow, Whittier,

Lowell, and Holmes. Some have written whole books of hymns: Bryant in this country, and in England not only Cowper but the present poet laureate, Dr. Bridges, who has even compiled a parish hymn book.

2. It would be a mistake to infer that because all of Cowper's sixty-eight Olney hymns were written by a poet they are all equally good. They are all spiritual and refined, and quite a number have proved useful. Some others seem like taskwork, and were perhaps written at Newton's request, to follow particular sermons of his in the Great House. The most famous of them is " There is a fountain filled with blood," in great favor among the older Evangelicals. Now it has become the fashion to criticize the imagery of its first verse as distasteful and not correctly interpreting Scripture.

Many would select as Cowper's best hymns, besides the one we are studying:

> " Hark, my soul, it is the Lord! "
> " O for a closer walk with God "
> " Sometimes a Light surprises "
> " Jesus, where'er Thy people meet "

with (for private use)

> " Far from the world, O Lord, I flee."

3. In *Olney Hymns,* " God moves in a mysterious way " is Number XV of the third " Book." Its title as there given is,

> " C.   Light shining out of darkness."

The " C " stands for Cowper's authorship, and the rest stands just as appropriately for his own experience. The text in *The Hymnal revised* is printed without change. Professor John E. B. Mayor lately found a commonplace book apparently in the handwriting of Cowper's first cousin, Maria, who married another cousin, Major William Cowper. It contains copies of letters and verses of Cowper and the fifth verse of this hymn ends:

> The bud may have a bitter taste,
> But wait to smell the flower.

Of the two readings, which is the better?

XIV

ALL HAIL THE POWER OF JESUS' NAME

THE TEXT OF THE HYMN

1 All hail the power of Jesus' Name!
   Let angels prostrate fall;
   Bring forth the royal diadem,
   And crown Him Lord of all.

2 Crown Him, ye morning stars of light,
   Who fixed this floating ball;
   Now hail the strength of Israel's might,
   And crown Him Lord of all.

3 Crown Him, ye martyrs of your God
   Who from His altar call;
   Extol the Stem of Jesse's rod,
   And crown Him Lord of all.

4 Ye seed of Israel's chosen race,
   Ye ransomed of the fall,
   Hail Him who saves you by His grace,
   And crown Him Lord of all.

5 Sinners, whose love can ne'er forget
   The wormwood and the gall,
   Go, spread your trophies at His feet,
   And crown Him Lord of all.

6 Let every kindred, every tribe,
   On this terrestrial ball,
   To Him all majesty ascribe,
   And crown Him Lord of all.

7 O that with yonder sacred throng
   We at His feet may fall;
   We'll join the everlasting song,
   And crown Him Lord of all.

Rev. Edward Perronet, 1779–80: verse 1, line 4 altered, verse
6 recast, verse 7 added by Rev. John Rippon, 1787

NOTE: The text of the hymn found in modern hymnals is based upon the altered form which Dr. John Rippon gave it in his Baptist *Selection of Hymns from the best Authors* published in 1787. The text from *The Hymnal revised*, as given above, is an attempt to embody as much of the original text as seemed practicable without causing confusion in congregations used to Rippon's arrangement.

As the original text is hard to come upon, it may be convenient to have it here as printed by Perronet himself in his *Occasional Verses, moral and sacred,* of 1785.

ON THE RESURRECTION.

I

ALL hail the power of JESU's name!
   Let Angels prostrate fall;
Bring forth the royal diadem,
   To crown Him LORD of All.

II

Let high-born Seraphs tune the lyre,
   And, as they tune it, fall
Before His face who tunes their choir,
   And crown Him LORD of All.

III

Crown Him, ye morning stars of light,
   Who fix'd this floating ball;
Now hail the strength of ISRAEL's might,
   And crown Him LORD of All.

IV

Crown Him, ye martyrs of your GOD,
   Who from His ALTAR call;
Extol the stem of JESSE's rod,
   And crown Him LORD of All.

V

Ye seed of ISRAEL's chosen race,
  Ye ransom'd of the fall,
Hail Him who saves you by His grace,
  And crown Him LORD of All.

VI

Hail Him, ye heirs of DAVID's line,
  Whom David LORD did call;
The GOD incarnate, man DIVINE;
  And crown Him LORD of All.

VII

SINNERS! whose love can ne'er forget
  The WORMWOOD and the GALL,
Go — spread your trophies at His feet,
  And crown Him LORD of All.

VIII

Let every tribe, and every tongue,
  That bound creation's call,
Now shout in universal song,
  THE CROWNED LORD OF ALL!

If one had a hymn or even a tune to contribute to the
common stock in the later years of the Evangelical Revival, he sent it in to *The Gospel Magazine,* which had
become the organ of the Calvinists. (It was there that
Toplady in 1776 printed his "Rock of Ages.") But it
was not quite the thing to sign your name to your hymn.
You gave a pen name, or perhaps none.

The Magazine for November, 1779, contained a tune
engraved in copperplate, to which was set a verse
beginning

"All hail the Pow'r of Jesu's Name."

One verse and no more. And not a sign as to who composed the tune or wrote the words. We know now that the composer was William Shrubsole, a young man of nineteen who had been a choir boy at the cathedral at Canterbury, and at the time was in London as a chapel organist. Shrubsole's tune at once attracted attention. That would naturally lead to inquiries for the remainder of the hymn. And in the April number of 1780 the whole hymn appeared in eight verses, with a footnote referring back to the tune, but without any clue as to the author.

WHO WROTE THE HYMN?

The editor of the Magazine must have been asked that question. If he knew, he did not publish his knowledge, and the authorship of the hymn remained a good deal of a puzzle for more than sixty years. It may be interesting now to arrange the pieces of the puzzle.

(1) In 1785 a little book appeared in London as *Occasional Verses, moral and sacred. Published for the instruction and amusement of the candidly serious and religious.* These productions, the preface says, " were not originally intended for public view, but occasionally shewn to a handful of friends ": one of whom has persuaded the author " to admit of their being made public " by his hands as " editor."

Among these verses, at page 22, is the hymn

"All hail the power of JESU's name!"

with the same text as in *The Gospel Magazine* five years earlier. To know the author of the book, then, was to find the writer of the hymn. But the book was not published and circulated by the book trade. It was printed privately " for the editor "; and outside the circle of the author's friends was very likely not even heard of.

(2) The hymn itself, however, had appeared in the Magazine at a time when Independents and Baptists had been singing Dr. Watts's hymns a long while, and were looking out for fresh hymns to add to them. As early as 1784 George Burder had taken this hymn into his *Collection of Hymns intended as a Supplement to Dr. Watts's Psalms and Hymns*. But he did not give the names of the authors of any of the hymns.

(3) In 1787 Dr. Rippon published his notable " Selection " as an Appendix to Dr. Watts. He included this hymn, with some changes and a new verse. He was a painstaking editor and sought to give the authors' names. But in this hymn he left a blank for the author's name, which evidently he did not know.

(4) In an edition of a hymn book called *Select Hymns and Anthems*, printed at Tunbridge-Wells about 1790, appeared a curious variation or revision of the hymn, beginning

> " All hail! the powers of Jesus' grace.
> Let angels prostrate fall:
> Bring forth the royal diadem,
> And crown him, Lord of all."

This was by " T. B." Now who was T. B.? Were these the initials of the original author, now presenting a revised version of his hymn? Or was T. B. a plagiarist, appropriating for his own materials that no one else had claimed? Neither the present writer nor his correspondents in England have been able to identify " T. B."

(5) In 1801 two Independent clergymen, Messrs. Williams and Boden, published *A Collection of Six Hundred Hymns* to supplement Watts. They copied this hymn from Rippon's book, but they filled Rippon's blank with " PERRONETT " as the author's name.

(6) John Dobell's *New Selection* of 1806 won a great success. In it he printed " All hail " with some changes. He gave the author's name as " Duncan." The Rev. John Duncan was a Scottish Presbyterian and one of four friends of Dobell who prefixed their " Recommendation " to his hymn book. Maybe Dr. Duncan had made a revised text of the hymn for his own use, and gave a manuscript copy to Dobell, who thought it Duncan's own. For some reason Duncan never had his own name erased in later editions of Dobell's book. And so a tradition arose that " All hail " was written by " Duncan." Among Dr. Duncan's own descendants the tradition merged into an established truth. On the strength of Dobell's authority, even the enlarged edition of Rippon's book, as late as 1844, inserted Duncan's name where Rippon himself had left a blank.

(7) In 1808 Thomas Young published his *Beauties of Dr. Watts, &c.* Young is said to have been the immediate successor of the Rev. Edward Perronet as pastor of a small dissenting congregation at Canterbury. It is further said that Young in his book attributes this hymn to his predecessor and also quotes from *Occasional Verses* of 1785 several pieces as Perronet's. The writer has a copy of *Beauties of Dr. Watts,* but not apparently the same book here referred to. He does not question these facts, but they are not within his knowledge. They seem to show that Young acted on personal or at least local information in ascribing this poem to Edward Perronet. His ascription certainly attracted little attention at the time.

(8) The hymn " All hail " came over to this country in copies of Dr. Rippon's hymn book of 1787, brought or sent here; the book itself being reprinted in New York

as early as 1792. And thus the hymn came with a blank space for the author's name. It caught the eye of Oliver Holden, a business man of Charlestown, Massachusetts, who was a self-taught musician and quite successful in composing hymn tunes in the florid style then in vogue.

THE ORGAN AT WHICH " CORONATION " WAS COMPOSED

He composed his jubilant " Coronation " for this hymn, and printed it in his *Union Harmony,* an oblong tune book in two volumes, published at Boston in 1793. From Holden's own copy, with the original copyright certificate pasted in, the present writer quotes the heading of the tune: " Coronation. C. M. Words by the Rev. Mr.

Medley." Samuel Medley was one of *The Gospel Magazine* circle of hymn writers. But why Holden selected
him for this honor is not clear. Nor is it important, as
Holden did not start a Medley tradition.

(9) The hymn came anew to this country in Dobell's
hymn book, reprinted here in 1810. With it came Duncan's name as author; and here the " Duncan " tradition
gained new currency. So that when the time came around
for American Presbyterians and Congregationalists to
make hymn books of their own, it was as the hymn of
" Duncan " that " All hail " went into them one by one.
Not that any of the editors had the least idea who or
what " Duncan " was.

(10) *The Evangelical Magazine* for December, 1858,
had a rather teasing communication from " J. K." of
Stepney, who seems to have met a son of one of Edward
Perronet's Canterbury friends. " We have before us,"
he says, " the hymn, ' All hail, &c.,' on a card printed
about 50 years since, at Canterbury, for the use of a
Sunday-school in that city, to which is appended the
following notice of the author, ' The Rev. Edward Perronet died at Canterbury, January 2, 1792.' " [His dying
words follow.]

" This is evidential," as the spiritualists say. But the
date is vague, and did the card say it was printed at
Canterbury, or did J. K's friend say that it was? J. K.
adds that " the copy of ' Occasional Verses ' " " now before us was presented by Mr. Perronet himself to the late
Mrs. Gellatly." But was the book so " autographed by
the author " ? Or was this only the remembered statement of " the late Mrs. Gellatly " ?

(11) In 1892 Dr. Julian's great *Dictionary of Hymnol-
ology* appeared. The annotator of this hymn is assured of

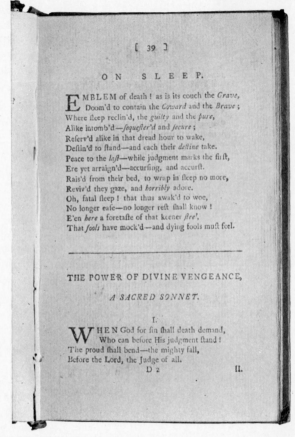

ON SLEEP.

EMBLEM of death ! as is its couch the *Grave*,
Doom'd to contain the *Coward* and the *Brave* ;
Where sleep reclin'd, the *guilty* and the *pure*,
Alike intomb'd—*sequester'd* and *secure* ;
Reserv'd alike in that dread hour to wake,
Destin'd to stand—and each their *destine* take.
Peace to the *last*—while judgment marks the first,
Ere yet arraign'd—accursing, and accurst.
Rais'd from their bed, to wrap in sleep no more,
Reviv'd they gaze, and *horribly* adore.
Oh, fatal sleep ! that thus awak'd to woe,
No longer ease—no longer rest shall know !
E'en *here* a foretaste of that keener *stee'*,
That *fools* have mock'd—and dying fools must feel.

THE POWER OF DIVINE VENGEANCE,

A SACRED SONNET.

I.

WHEN God for sin shall death demand,
Who can before His judgment stand !
The proud shall bend—the mighty fall,
Before the Lord, the Judge of all.

D 2

II.

THE SOLUTION OF THE PUZZLE AS TO AUTHORSHIP

Perronet's authorship. But apparently he had not heard of J. K. The only actual proofs he offers are (a) that one piece in *Occasional Verses* is dedicated to the memory of Vincent Perronet, who was Edward's father, and others " apparently to various members of his family, who are indicated by their initials only "; and (b) that the copy of *Occasional Verses* in the British Museum is bound up with two poetical pamphlets, one of them bearing Perronet's signature, while the other " may also be ascribed to him with certainty."

(12) When the writer began to prepare this study he examined the grounds of his own faith in Perronet's authorship of " All hail." " Is the evidence of it complete and satisfying? " he asked himself. He had to acknowledge that it was not.

The writer made up his mind to examine his copy of *Occasional Verses* minutely for some further clue of authorship. This he did without result up to page 201. There he found that the verses in memory of C. P. and D. P. were acrostics. The first letter of each line of the former, read downward, spelled Charles Perronet, and those of the second spelled Damaris Perronet — Edward's brother and sister. Then the writer knew what further to look for, and found it on page 39; an acrostic revealing Edward Perronet's own name.

This little discovery seems to settle the matter finally. Perronet acknowledged his authorship of the book and the hymn in his own way. Doubtless he did not expect to wait one hundred and twenty-six years for his acknowledgement to be discovered.

We can now see easily enough how things happened as they did. Shrubsole was living in the same city of Canterbury as Perronet, and was no doubt one of the friends to whom Perronet showed or gave a manuscript copy of his hymn. Shrubsole liked it and set it to music which he sent to *The Gospel Magazine* for publication. And when the remainder of the hymn was asked for he turned in his own copy or got one from the author.

THE AUTHOR OF THE HYMN

There was probably no Church of England clergyman whom the Wesleys relied on so much as Vincent Perronet, Vicar of Shoreham, in Kent. He was a gentle and studious saint, son of a French refugee and retaining the French charm of manner. His son Edward, born in 1721, was brought up in the Church and fully intended to enter its ministry, but, under the influence of the Wesleys, became a Methodist traveling preacher. He started out at once to accompany Charles Wesley on a preaching tour. " He got a deal of abuse thereby, and not a little dirt," Charles said, " both which he took very patiently."

Perronet seems to have been a bold and successful preacher and a man of undoubted piety. But he was impulsive and restless under the control of the Wesleys, and soon began to make trouble for them. Visiting from house to house he would criticize them, especially their refusal to allow their preachers to administer the sacraments. He developed an acrid antipathy to the Church of England, and in 1756 published a satire in verse, *The Mitre,* ridiculing episcopal government and priestly pretension. It was a grief to his father and a serious matter for the Wesleys. And among them they persuaded Perronet to suppress it. He must have given away some copies, for a few still survive.

Later he left the Methodists and became a preacher in the Countess of Huntingdon's Connexion. But she, too, remonstrated against his bitterness toward the Church. He left her and became pastor of a small dissenting meeting in Canterbury, where he preached until his death on January 8, 1792. He was buried in the cloister of the famous cathedral.

And so closed obscurely just such a career as may be worked out by a good man of no commanding gifts, with an irascible temper, an impatience of authority, and a touch of bitterness that grows with " not being understood." His hymn is the one achievement of his life. It breaks through the crusty manner of an unappreciated and disappointed man, and reveals him as one that had " such exalted views of the Lord Jesus, and so completely enthroned Him in his thoughts and affections."

SOME POINTS FOR DISCUSSION

1. In *The Gospel Magazine* the hymn was entitled " On the Resurrection. The Lord is King." Hence the opening " All hail ": the risen Lord's salutation on the resurrection morning according to Matt. 28:9. And the angels were first to proclaim him. But is the hymn really an appropriate Easter hymn?

2. This hymn is a religious song rather than a religious poem. Its structure makes it very monotonous to read. But its structure makes it also very effective for singing; each verse beginning afresh and mounting to the fullchorded refrain. Perhaps no other hymn is quite so jubilant and triumphant. It has become very dear to the heart of the Church, and, if sung reverently, can hardly fail to warm that heart. It is of course possible

to use it, like firecrackers, for the sake of making a noise at a festival.

3. A strain from Shrubsole's tune (it has long been called " Miles Lane ") is carved on his tombstone at Bunhill Fields, London. A verse of the hymn is engraved on Oliver Holden's tomb in the old Burying Ground at Charlestown. In England the hymn has been inseparable from Shrubsole's tune. In this country it has been inseparable from Holden's. Both tunes are printed in *The Hymnal revised*. Both are a part of the history of the hymn; and having both we are at liberty to choose between them.

XV

O GOD OF BETHEL, BY WHOSE HAND

THE TEXT OF THE HYMN

1   O God of Bethel, by whose hand
     Thy people still are fed,
   Who through this weary pilgrimage
     Hast all our fathers led,

2   Our vows, our prayers, we now present
     Before Thy throne of grace;
   God of our fathers, be the God
     Of their succeeding race.

3   Through each perplexing path of life
     Our wandering footsteps guide
   Give us each day our daily bread,
     And raiment fit provide.

4   O spread Thy covering wings around
     Till all our wanderings cease,
   And at our Father's loved abode
     Our souls arrive in peace.

5   Such blessings from Thy gracious hand
     Our humble prayers implore;
   And Thou shalt be our chosen God
     And portion evermore.

Verses 1–4 by Rev. Philip Doddridge, 1737, recast by Rev.
John Logan, 1781: verse 1, line 1, altered, and verse 5 added
in Scottish *Translations and Paraphrases*, 1781

NOTE: There are three texts of this hymn:

1. Doddridge's original text of 173% as hereinafter printed. From this the hymn went into the *Translations and Paraphrases* of 1745, with trifling changes. This is the first printed text.

2. The text given by Job Orton in his collection of Doddridge's hymns (1755), opening with "O God of Jacob." The changes in J. D. Humphrey's 1839 edition of the hymns may be passed over.

3. The recast made by the Rev. John Logan, printed (with some variances) in his *Poems* and in the *Translations and Paraphrases*, both of 1781. It is the latter text (given above) that has become so familiar.

This and the other hymns of Dr. Doddridge belong to the period of the eighteenth century revival but are scarcely of it. They run rather with the stream of hymn singing and hymn writing among English Independents, of which Dr. Watts was the fountainhead. Hymnologists say that Doddridge is one of "the school of Watts." They mean that Watts's hymns became so much the pattern for other hymn writers that he was like a schoolmaster giving out specimens of penmanship to be imitated; and that Doddridge was one of the imitators. But he was head boy in the school, and his hymns came to be regarded as a desirable addition even to those of his master.

The hymn we are now studying won by its own merits a place in the wider spreading movement to allow the singing of human hymns. For when that movement reached even Psalm-loving Scotland, this was one of the " Paraphrases " selected by the General Assembly in 1781 and recommended to the churches.

"THE GOOD DR. DODDRIDGE"

In some " unknown house in the labyrinth of London streets " Philip Doddridge was born in the summer of

1702. It was a humble home and a very sickly baby. His earliest recollection was of his mother explaining the scenes of Bible history pictured on the blue-and-white Dutch tiles lining the fireplace: Eve's apple tree with the serpent, Noah at the window of the ark, a very large Jonah coming forth from a very small whale, Peter crossing the Sea of Galilee in a Dutch three-decker, the prodigal son in a periwig, and the rest. She would tell him of her father, driven from his Bohemian home by religious persecution, and show him the Luther's Bible in black stamped leather he brought away beneath the peasant clothes he wore; of his father's father also, one of the Church of England clergy ejected in 1662 for conscience' sake.

Both father and mother died while Philip was a child at Kingston grammar school. Sent to another school at St. Albans, he won the notice of Dr. Samuel Clark, the Presbyterian pastor, who befriended him and admitted him to the Communion at nineteen. He went up to London to seek encouragement toward preparing for the ministry. The Duchess of Bedford offered to finance him, but only if he would conform to the established Church. The dissenting leaders were cold. Dr. Clark called him back, and sent him to be trained by John Jennings, at Kibworth, where he was happy in his books and content in his poverty. In 1723 he was qualified to preach by the county meeting of ministers, and became pastor at out-of-the-way Kibworth, where, he said, " I have not so much as a tea table in my whole diocese and but one hoop petticoat within the whole circuit "; but where he could spend twelve hours a day in his study. Doddridge's chance came at Market Harborough, to which he had moved, when the Independents decided to

DR. PHILIP DODDRIDGE

set up an academy there and selected him as principal.
Only twenty-six years old, he consulted Dr. Watts, then
fifty-four, and thus began a warm friendship with the
great man. Very shortly he was called to a larger church
at Northampton. He took his academy with him and
made it famous; spending the rest of his life there as
teacher, pastor, and author.

In Doddridge's time " the dissenting interest " was on
the down grade. Its heroic age was past: easy days
brought easy ways and spiritual indifference. Dr. Watts
and other Nonconformist leaders were as much opposed
to " enthusiasm " as were the bishops themselves. They
turned their backs on the revival and scorned the Wesleys
and Whitefield. The kindly Doddridge, when he got
to know them better, could not keep it up. In London,
one day in 1743, he even led in public prayer at Whitefield's Tabernacle. Whereupon Dr. Watts wrote him
that many of his friends were asking an explanation of
his " sinking the character of a minister and especially
of a tutor among the dissenters, so low thereby." When
later he had Whitefield to preach from his Northampton
pulpit, a very storm of protest and reproach rained on
him: all of which only strengthened the stand he
had taken. He was the first Nonconformist leader to
hold out a brotherly hand to the great evangelists.

Doddridge's one aim in all his laborious ministry was
to deepen the spiritual life, not only among dissenters
but in general society. To this practical end his many
books were written. His *Rise and Progress of Religion
in the Soul* became something like a religious classic.
The Family Expositor, covering all the New Testament,
took twelve years of his life and was greatly esteemed in
its day. He disliked controversy and liked a theology

emphasizing the statements of Scripture rather than the definitions of the schools. In a controversial age this led some to question the straitness of his orthodoxy. Nobody ever questioned his loving-kindness.

He was not a great writer and probably not a great preacher. He could not stay the decline of dissent even in his own parish. But he did good service in many ways: the more easily because in spite of bodily weakness and consumptive tendencies he had a healthy mind, a heart full of God's sunshine, and pleasant ways. Perhaps he helped the most simply by being so lovable, for to love a good man is a big step in anybody's religious education. Many hearts followed him on his voyage to Lisbon in the autumn of 1751, made possible by the bounty of Lady Huntingdon and other friends. " I can as well go to Heaven from Lisbon as from my own study at Northampton," he told her at parting. The study at Northampton is still kept just as he left it, and at Lisbon his body still lies in the English cemetery, near the grave of the great novelist, Henry Fielding.

THE STORY OF THE HYMN

Doddridge's " works " gather dust on the shelves; some of his hymns are in familiar use. Like those of Davies and other eighteenth century preachers they were written in the glow of sermon composition to be sung at the sermon's close. " O God of Bethel " was to follow a sermon on " Jacob's Vow," from Genesis 28:20-22. During his life his hymns were more or less handed about in manuscript. Four years after his death his friend Job Orton copied three hundred and seventy of them from his papers and published them as *Hymns founded on various texts in the Holy Scriptures. By the late Philip Doddridge, D.D.* [1755.] Others have been published since and some are yet unprinted. In Orton's book this hymn begins, "O God of Jacob." The earliest form known is that dated "Jan. 16, 173$\frac{6}{7}$" in Doddridge's own handwriting, which the present writer has not seen. Dr. Julian, who has, gives it thus:

1

Oh God of Bethel, by whose Hand
Thine Israel still is fed
Who thro' this weary Pilgrimage
Hast all our Fathers led

2

To thee our humble Vows we raise
To thee address our Prayer
And in thy kind and faithful Breast
Deposite all our Care

3

If thou thro' each perplexing Path
Wilt be our constant Guide
If thou wilt daily Bread supply
And Raiment wilt provide

4

If thou wilt spread thy Shield around
Till these our wandrings cease
And at our Father's lov'd Abode
Our Souls arrive in Peace

5

To thee as to our Covenant God
We'll our whole selves resign
And count that not our tenth alone
But all we have is thine.

So much for Dr. Doddridge and the hymn as he wrote it. Its further study carries us over into Presbyterian Scotland.

THE SCOTTISH " PARAPHRASES "

In our study of " The Lord's my Shepherd, I'll not want," we saw how Calvin's ideal of singing " the Bible only " conquered Scotland at the Reformation, and made its Church a Psalm singing Church; how at the time of the Westminster Assembly a new version of " The Psalms of David in meeter " was adopted; and how fond Scottish hearts became of that " Rous's Version." But as Dr. Watts's more evangelical renderings of Psalms and his hymns came to be known they caused a certain restlessness and on the part of many ministers a desire for liberty to sing them or something like them in church. Nevertheless the men who made the first proposals to change the established usage of the Scottish people must have had hopeful temperaments. Time and again when a movement " to enlarge the Psalmody " came to the surface in the General Assembly it was quietly sidetracked.

The Assembly of 1741 pigeonholed a petition that other passages of Scripture in meter be added to the Psalms. Next year a persistent presbytery called it up. They succeeded in getting a committee appointed to gather materials and in putting such pressure on the committee that after four years it laid before the Assembly of 1745 a meager collection of forty-five *Translations and Paraphrases of several passages of Sacred Scripture,* nineteen of them taken from Dr. Watts. This had to go down to the presbyteries for their approval. Then followed a contest in which the innovators kept

Tranflations and Paraphrafes,

IN VERSE,

Of feveral Paffages of

SACRED SCRIPTURE.

Collected and prepared by a Committee of the
General Affembly of the Church of Scotland, in order to be fung in Churches.

NEC TAMEN CONSUMEBATUR

EDINBURGH:
Printed and fold by J. Dickson,
Printer to the Church of Scotland.
MDCCLXXXI.

THE FIRST HYMN BOOK OF PRESBYTERIAN SCOTLAND

the little book for ten years before the General Assembly, where they always seemed to be winning, only to be baffled by the lovers of the old Psalms in the presbyteries. These standfasts saw to it that enough of the presbyteries refrained year after year from taking any action, until the patience of the innovators was worn out and their project abandoned.

Twenty years passed before it was renewed, and six more before a new collection of sixty-seven " paraphrases " and five " hymns " was ready to be sent down for the presbyteries to report upon. That was in 1781, and the Assembly gave the churches leave to sing them while the matter was pending. The old tactics were resumed, and so many presbyteries ignored the new book also that no further action could be taken by the Assembly. But perhaps the standfasts overreached themselves this time, since the failure to take final action upon the Paraphrases extended indefinitely the permission already given to sing them pending such action. In this way the little book, whose title page is before us, became the first hymn book of Scottish Presbyterianism: it made the first breach in the old Psalmody.

In some parishes bitter feeling and disturbances followed when a minister attempted to have the new Paraphrases sung. There were, however, many ministers who never gave them out until their life's end; and the outraged feelings of many plain people have a monument in Scottish Bibles still preserved in which the leaves containing the Paraphrases are carefully pasted down or from which they are torn out. But in the end they fairly won their place beside the Psalms and became almost as dear to the people.

" O God of Bethel " is the second of the Paraphrases

of 1781, but holds the first place in Scottish hearts. In illustration of this it is worth while to quote a charming letter which Samuel R. Crockett, the novelist, sent in response to Mr. W. T. Stead's inquiry for " the hymns that have helped " him: —

" One hymn I love, and that (to be Irish) is not a hymn, but what in our country is mystically termed a ' paraphrase.' It is that which, when sung to the tune of St. Paul's, makes men and women square themselves and stand erect to sing, like an army that goes gladly to battle: ' O God of Bethel ' —

" I wish I could quote it all. Of course it is in vain to try to tell what these songs of ' Christ's ain Kirk and Covenant ' are to us who sucked them in with our mother-milk and heard them crooned for cradle songs to ' Coleshill ' and ' Kilmarnock.' But be assured that whatever new songs are written, noble and sincere, there will always be a number who will walk in the old paths, and, by choice, seek for their ' helping ' (about which they will mostly keep silence) from the songs their fathers sang."

But the use of this paraphrase is not confined to Scotland. It has crossed the border and become as familiar in England as in Scotland. It was sung in Westminster Abbey in 1874 at the public funeral of David Livingstone, the great African missionary and traveler, and again in 1879 at the funeral of Lord Lawrence, Governor-General of India. And the biographers of both men refer to the impressiveness of the simple words, as sung to the music of Tallis. In this country and in Canada the Scottish immigration would of itself insure a widespread use of the paraphrase.

SOME POINTS FOR DISCUSSION

1. No doubt the quaint title, *Translations and Paraphrases*, was originally intended to conciliate those still holding to the Calvinistic position that the inspired words of Scripture should furnish the only " subject-matter of praise." And yet it is hard to believe that such camouflage could deceive a people so keen-eyed in searching the Scripture. " O God of Bethel," for instance. It certainly is not a " translation " of the passage in Genesis on which it is based; but could it in any sense be regarded as a " paraphrase " of that passage, or is it simply a free human hymn?

2. The committee who prepared the *Translations and Paraphrases* of 1745 procured a copy of Doddridge's hymn in manuscript (it had not appeared in print as yet), and they adopted it with very few alterations. The committee of 1781, on the other hand, made a great many, as may be seen by comparing their text (*The Hymnal revised*, No. 533) with the original as quoted above. These amendments were doubtless made by the Rev. John Logan, a member of the committee with a deft hand at verse-making but of questionable character, to say the least. Let us hope it was only an exaggerated sense of the value of his improvements of Doddridge's hymn that led him to print this paraphrase as his own among his *Poems* of that same year, 1781.

Modern feeling runs strongly against the practice of " tinkering " hymns, as was done so freely by the committee of 1781, and in favor of singing them as their authors wrote them. In the case of this paraphrase a modern editor of a hymn book has to choose whether to adopt the 1781 text or to go back to the original. If he is a good editor he will probably say (1) that Logan's text is in many ways better than Doddridge's; (2) that the hymn as Doddridge wrote it is practically unknown, and, as Logan altered it, widely loved; and, if he is editing a Presbyterian hymn book, he will probably add (3) that the form in which the hymn appeared in the Paraphrases of 1781 is the accepted text of what must be recognized as one of the historic hymns of Presbyterianism.

3. In Scotland, " O God of Bethel " is still sung to " St. Paul," of which Mr. Crockett wrote, a tune that dates from 1749; sometimes to the older tune known there as " French " and here as " Dundee." In Westminster Abbey it is still sung to the sixteenth century tune known as " Tallis's Ordinal " or simply " Tallis." " Balerma," to which the words are set in *The Hymnal revised,* is also Scottish, an arrangement dating only from 1833, and is probably more acceptable to American congregations than the older and graver tunes.

4. Of the thirteen hymns of Doddridge in *The Hymnal revised,* " Hark the glad sound! the Saviour comes " and " Jesus, I love Thy charming Name " seem to have most of his vitality; " How gentle God's commands," and " See Israel's gentle Shepherd stand " most of his tenderness. Queen Victoria's husband thought so much of " O happy day that fixed my choice " that he had it sung at the confirmations of their children. In this country it has become associated (perhaps indissolubly) with an old-time camp-meeting melody, carrying a jingle-like refrain, with which many good people would not care to express their praise. Toward the close of the eighteenth century, by some agency as yet undiscovered, " My

God, and is Thy table spread " got itself bound up with a few other hymns at the end of Church of England prayer books, and it has been a favorite Communion hymn ever since. To the writer it seems more appropriate to those who stay away from the sacrament.

And there are a few more of the thirteen that raise in his mind a question whether they may not have outlived their usefulness. Each generation develops its own natural religious idiom, and it may be that Doddridge's " Lord of the Sabbath, hear us pray " and " Grace! 'tis a charming sound," came more naturally from the lips of his generation than they do from ours.

XVI

HAIL TO THE LORD'S ANOINTED

THE TEXT OF THE HYMN

1 Hail to the Lord's Anointed,
   Great David's greater Son!
Hail, in the time appointed,
   His reign on earth begun!
He comes to break oppression,
   To set the captive free,
To take away transgression,
   And rule in equity.

2 He shall come down like showers
   Upon the fruitful earth;
And love, joy, hope, like flowers,
   Spring in His path to birth;
Before Him on the mountains
   Shall peace, the herald, go,
And righteousness, in fountains,
   From hill to valley flow.

3 Kings shall fall down before Him,
   And gold and incense bring;
All nations shall adore Him,
   His praise all people sing;
For Him shall prayer unceasing
   And daily vows ascend;
His kingdom still increasing,
   A kingdom without end.

4 O'er every foe victorious,
   He on His throne shall rest,
From age to age more glorious,
   All blessing and all-blest:

> The tide of time shall never
> His covenant remove,
> His name shall stand for ever, —
> That Name to us is Love.

James Montgomery's version of the Seventy-second Psalm,
written in 1821

NOTE: The above text is an abridgment of the original, which was in eight verses as printed in *Songs of Zion*, 1822.

In taking up this hymn of James Montgomery we pass over into the nineteenth century. And so we leave behind us the eighteenth century hymns — of Watts and his followers on the one side and of the Wesleys and other singers of the great revival on the other.

It was of course from those eighteenth century stores that our American Churches, whether Evangelical or Unitarian, had to draw as they began to make hymn books of their own. Now the dominant note of those hymns is personal piety. It is interesting and in a way touching to remember how the heart of our witty Boston poet, Oliver Wendell Holmes, a rather radical Unitarian, turned back in his old age to those eighteenth century hymns. He perceived in them " the old ring of saintliness " and a virility he missed in modern hymns. " When I turn to the hymn book, and when one strikes my eye, I cover the name at the bottom and guess. It is," he said, " almost invariably by Watts or Wesley; after them there are very few which are good for much."

Perhaps the Unitarian hymn book which the poet had in his gallery pew at King's Chapel failed to do justice to the later hymn writers, choosing those that gave out the ring of modern liberalism rather than " the old ring of saintliness." However that may be, most Christians will not believe that deep and sincere piety passed away with the eighteenth century or that the true succession of God's singing men has been broken off.

When the nineteenth century dawned, the voices of all the great hymn writers had passed into silence. Watts and Doddridge had been dead for the half, Toplady for the quarter of a century. The Wesleys had been dead for a decade; Cowper had just died; only Newton survived in the weakness of old age. But with the early

THE CHAPEL COTTAGE WHERE JAMES MONTGOMERY WAS BORN, IN IRVINE, SCOTLAND

years of the new century a new hymn writer appeared, worthy to take his place in the great succession. This was James Montgomery, a Moravian layman; a poor boy with nothing to depend on but his literary talent; a forward-looking man who kept abreast of the marked religious progress of his time; a poet who could not only sing over the old songs of Zion with a fresh and clear voice but could also furnish new songs for new occasions.

THE AUTHOR OF THE HYMN

Shortly after writing " Children of the heavenly King," John Cennick started a little Moravian settlement in the county of Antrim, Ireland. Among the neighbors who joined it was John Montgomery, apparently a laborer, who for some gift or grace was made a Moravian preacher and sent over to Irvine on the Scottish coast. There, on November 4, 1771, in a cottage adjoining the Moravian chapel, his son James was born; "narrowly escaping," he used afterwards to say, " being an Irishman." When the parents went as missionaries to the West Indies they left the boy at the Moravian school at Fulneck, near Leeds, and took with them the hope that he would prepare himself for the ministry.

It was a very severe school, as closely guarded against the world as a convent, with most of the world's literature forbidden. Dr. Blair's poem, " The Grave," was an exception, and hearing it read started Montgomery's poetic impulse, just as the quaint Moravian hymn book in constant use started his lifelong interest in hymns. He neglected the prescribed studies and spent his time in composing epics in Milton's manner. The Brethren gave him up as a candidate for the ministry and put him in a baker's shop as shopboy.

The lad became very unhappy there and at the age of sixteen ran away, to begin the world with three shillings and six and a bundle of poems in his pocket. It was characteristic of him that he went off in his old suit, leaving behind him a new one which his master had given him, and which he did not think he had earned. And it was no doubt humiliating to him that he had to ask his

James Montgomery.

old teachers at Fulneck for a recommendation before he
could get even a situation in another shop in the village
of Wath. This also he left after a year and went up to
London with a larger bundle of poems in his pocket and
the vision of a publisher ready to print them. When that
hope failed, he went back to his situation at Wath.

One day in his twenty-second year he saw in a radical
newspaper, *The Sheffield Register,* its publisher's adver-
tisement for a clerk. He answered it in person and secured the place. He began to exercise his literary talent
in the paper, and, when its proprietor and editor had to
flee from political prosecution, a fellow townsman found
the means of carrying it on, and put Montgomery in
charge. It was an exciting time in politics, and a critical
situation for the young editor of a suspected sheet. The
skies were lurid with reflections of the flames of the
French Revolution. Sheffield was in the thickest of the
conflict between the aristocrats and the Jacobins. And
amidst all the clamor for the rights of man, the government was insistently trying to raise recruits for the expected war with France.

The ardent young editor's sympathies were with the
democrats, and he was eager for parliamentary reform,
to say the least. Almost at once he was arrested for
printing a seditious ballad and put in jail for three
months. A few months after his release he was charged
with seditious libel for an account he printed of the manner in which the military commander had put down a
riot in the streets, was found guilty, and imprisoned once
more for six months. He spent his enforced leisure in
jail in composing poetry, afterwards printed as *Prison
Amusements.* On coming out he resumed his editorship
and kept it up until 1825. But at heart he was neither

a politician nor a newspaper man, but a poet, and
through these years he gave more thought to poetry than
to making the most of his newspaper. It was his old Fulneck School scheme of life over again, and not the way
that leads to fortune; but Montgomery was unmarried
and free to follow the gleam.

As calmer times came, Montgomery's own opinions became mellower, and his increasing poetic reputation reflected luster on Sheffield. The simple goodness of the
man and his unfailing helpfulness in every worthy cause
conquered all hearts. He became recognized as the first
citizen of the town, and the government that had twice
jailed him put him on its pension list. And so he spent
his last years contentedly and helpfully, esteemed by all
as the best of men and by many as a great poet. He had
not been without his struggles to gain a place, but he
bore no grudge against life, except perhaps at the persis-
tency with which many people confused his personality
with that of a namesake whose poetry he did not admire.

Dr. Theodore L. Cuyler, of Brooklyn, visited him in
1842. "A short, brisk, cheery old man, then seventy-one,
came into the room with a spry step. He wore a suit
of black, with old-fashioned dress ruffles, and a high
cravat that looked as if it choked him. His complexion
was fresh, and snowy hair crowned a noble forehead. We
chatted about America, and I told him that in all our
churches his hymns were great favorites. I unfortunately happened to mention that when lately in Glasgow
I had gone to hear the Rev. Robert Montgomery, the author of ' Satan,' and other poems. It was this ' Satan
Montgomery ' whom Macaulay had scalped with merci-
less criticism in the *Edinburgh Review*. The mention of
his name aroused the old poet's ire. ' Would you believe

it?' he exclaimed indignantly, 'they attribute some of that fellow's performances to me, and lately a lady wrote me in reference to one of his most pompous poems, and said it was the best that I had ever written!'"

The poet (James, not Robert) had arranged to spend the Easter of 1854 with his brethren at Fulneck, was unable to go, and on April 30 was dead. He was buried with such a funeral as Sheffield had never seen, and in the years following two of his friends with great devotion but less judgment published a biography extending to no less than seven volumes.

MONTGOMERY AS POET AND HYMN WRITER

It is just as well that a popular poet should die before his reputation begins to fade, and Montgomery's had lasted a good while. The first of his poems to catch the public ear was his *Wanderer in Switzerland* of 1806, of which three editions were called for. Volume after volume followed, the series closing with the long poem of *The Pelican Island* of 1826 and the short pieces collected in *The Poet's Portfolio* of 1835. They all appealed to a large public, mostly the religious public who valued such pure sentiments in the vesture of verse they could read and understand. But the longer poems have found no place in English literature, and the anthologies preserve none of his lyrics except a few hymns. And this is just as it ought to be. In his poetic work Montgomery mistook the easy flow of rhetorical or sentimental verse for poetry. But his hymn writing was a thing apart, and in the best of his hymns he made no mistake of any kind. He understood exactly what to aim at, and he is one of " the little masters " in the art of hymn writing.

As early as 1822 Montgomery gathered his versions of Psalms, including the one now before us, in his *Songs of Zion.* He printed many of his hymns in a collection called *The Christian Psalmist,* in 1825; and at the last gathered up the hymns of a lifetime in the *Original Hymns* of 1853. He wrote four hundred in all, of which not less than a hundred have had a part in the worship of some branch of the Church.

THE STORY OF THE HYMN

Many have regarded this as the best of all, and at the present time it is found in more hymn books than anything else of Montgomery's. And it has something of a story.

It was written to be sung at a Christmas festival of 1821, at one of the Moravian settlements in England, Fulneck probably. Which reminds us that Montgomery was a Moravian all his life, though he did not formally resume his birthright membership until his forty-third birthday. In January, 1822, he inclosed a copy of the hymn in a letter to a South Sea missionary, suggesting that the isles afar are to share the glories of the Messianic reign. In April of that year it was recited by the author at a great Methodist missionary meeting at Liverpool, under rather striking circumstances. The lights went out while he was speaking, a crash resounded from a seat back broken by the crowd, and it was uncertain what might happen. The chairman called out, " There is still light within." The speaker took his cue, proceeded not without agitation, " concluding with the full blaze of the renovated illumination " by reciting his " Hail to the Lord's Anointed." And we can imagine that it was not

spoken or heard without a perceptible thrill. Dr. Adam
Clarke, who presided at the meeting, was so impressed
that he secured a copy, and in 1822 appended the hymn
to his notes on the Seventy-second Psalm in his now
famous *Commentary on the Bible,* with a special note
calling attention to its excellence; which no doubt contributed a good deal to the hymn's success.

SOME POINTS FOR DISCUSSION

1. In Montgomery's *Original Hymns* this bears the
title,

" The Reign of Christ on Earth. — Ps. lxxii,"

and it is of course a free rendering of that Psalm. The
Seventy-second Psalm is the vision of a great king who
brings righteousness and peace, redresses human wrongs,
and extends his rule to the world's end. The Old Testament seems to apply the Psalm to Solomon's reign, and
the New Testament does not apply it to Christ as Messianic King. The Early Church did, and chose it as the
special Psalm for the Epiphany season. Now just what
did they mean by that?

The Epiphany (January 6) follows so soon after
Christmas that many people think of them as one. It
really commemorates the visit of the Wise Men, and
when the Church put the Psalm in that connection it
meant to say that it foretells the homage of the nations
to Christ, of which the visit of the Wise Men was the
beginning. What the Church did then was to choose the
Seventy-second as its special foreign missionary Psalm.

The nineteenth century Churches have done just the
same thing with Montgomery's rendering of that Psalm.

For a Meeting of Christian Ministers.

Pour out the Spirit from on high;
Lord, thine assembled Servants bless;
Graces and gifts to each supply,
And clothe thy Priests with righteousness.

Before thine altar when we stand,
To teach the truth as taught by thee,
Saviour, like Stars in thy right-hand,
The Angels of thy Churches be.

Wisdom, and zeal, and faith impart,
Firmness with meekness, from above,
— To bear thy people on our heart,
And love the Souls whom thou dost love.—

To watch and pray, and never faint,
By day and night, strict guard to keep;
To warn the sinner, cheer the saint,
Nourish thy Lambs and feed thy sheep.—

Then, when our work is finish'd here,
In humble hope our charge resign;
— When the Chief Shepherd shall appear,
O God! may they and we be thine.

J. Montgomery

AN AUTOGRAPH HYMN OF MONTGOMERY

They have always regarded it as a foreign missionary hymn, a trumpet call to advance toward the conquest of the world, a blessed assurance of victory. We may be quite sure that the author so intended it. He wrote in the early glow of the new zeal for foreign missions that dawned on England, and which so moved his heart. Is the Church justified in making this hymn a song of the final triumph of foreign missions; and just what bearing upon this question has the old saying, " My kingdom is not of this world? "

2. There are no differences of text in this hymn as printed in *Songs of Zion* in 1822 and in *Original Hymns,* thirty-one years later. The fact is worth noting, as a number of editors have made changes, especially in the last line. But as Montgomery printed the hymn, there were eight verses of eight lines each; not too many for a proper presentation of the Psalm but too many for a congregational hymn book; so that each editor has to decide on his own abridgment. That in *The Hymnal revised* is perhaps as effective as any; the best of the omitted verses, the original second, is rather a loss:

> He comes with succour speedy,
>   To those who suffer wrong;
> To help the poor and needy,
>   And bid the weak be strong:
> To give them songs for sighing,
>   Their darkness turn to light;
> Whose souls, condemn'd and dying,
>   Were precious in His sight.

3. What is the meaning of " For Him shall prayer unceasing," in the third verse, regarded by some as an improper expression? Does the fact that the Seventy-

second Psalm is itself a prayer for the king bear upon the questioned propriety of the expression?

4. Another and equally well-known missionary hymn, " Jesus shall reign where'er the sun," is also a version of the Seventy-second Psalm, written in Dr. Watts's very best style. And it may be interesting to compare the work of two excellent hymn writers dealing with the same subject matter a century apart. Dr. Watts would probably have regarded Montgomery's meter and rhythm as a bit jaunty for a hymn.

XVII

JUST AS I AM, WITHOUT ONE PLEA

THE TEXT OF THE HYMN

1 Just as I am, without one plea
   But that Thy blood was shed for me,
   And that Thou bidd'st me come to Thee,
     O Lamb of God, I come.

2 Just as I am, and waiting not
   To rid my soul of one dark blot,
   To Thee, whose blood can cleanse each spot,
     O Lamb of God, I come.

3 Just as I am, though tossed about
   With many a conflict, many a doubt,
   Fightings and fears within, without,
     O Lamb of God, I come.

4 Just as I am, poor, wretched, blind;
   Sight, riches, healing of the mind,
   Yea, all I need, in Thee to find,
     O Lamb of God, I come.

5 Just as I am! Thou wilt receive,
   Wilt welcome, pardon, cleanse, relieve;
   Because Thy promise I believe,
     O Lamb of God, I come.

6 Just as I am! Thy love unknown
   Has broken every barrier down;
   Now, to be Thine, yea, Thine alone,
     O Lamb of God, I come.

Charlotte Elliott, *circa* 1834

NOTE: The text is taken from the 1841 edition of *The Invalid's Hymn Book*. The only changes are (1) In *punctuation:* by eliminating an exclamation point at the end of each verse; and also dashes, the position and number of which vary in Miss Elliott's printings of her hymn. Her final use of them was to make a light parenthesis of all between " Just as I am " and " O Lamb of God ": in verse 1 for example, " Just as I am — " . . . . " Come to Thee — ." (2) In *text:* In 1841 verse 3, l. 3, reads, " Fightings within, and fears without," within quotation marks. Quoting, no doubt, John Newton (from memory) and discovering verbal inaccuracy, she changed the line to read (as in *Hours of Sorrow,* ed. 1849, and her collected poems) as given above.

In these studies we have had occasion more than once to refer to the Evangelical Party in the Church of England. It was the succession of clergy and laity who continued to believe the doctrines of the Evangelical or Calvinistic side of the eighteenth century revival, and who carried out its principles in their parish work, as far as they could. That Evangelical succession in the Church of England has never failed yet. Its characteristic might be expressed broadly by saying that it puts the gospel first and the Church second, so that it is generally called the Low Church Party.

There never was anybody more directly in the line of that succession than Miss Charlotte Elliott, the author of " Just as I am." It was her heritage from a line of Evangelical clergymen; she was born into a home that was the center of a prominent Evangelical circle; she was nurtured in the doctrines not only by her parents but by an uncle and two brothers who were Evangelical clergymen; and when she began to write hymns she took her place at once in the succession of Evangelical hymn writers, after Toplady and Newton and Cowper. Her hymn, " Just as I am," is a clear expression of what the

Evangelical Party believed as to the doctrine of salvation, and what it stood for as opposing High Church or
Broad Church doctrines. She thought of the Church
simply as " The Church of pardoned sinners," and it
was a sorrow to her to see one and another friend or
relative turn to what we call High Church views but
which she used to characterize as " Puseyite errors."

THE AUTHOR OF "JUST AS I AM"

Charlotte Elliott's parents were gentlefolk in very
comfortable circumstances, who had homes at Clapham
and Brighton, and she was born at Brighton, March 17,
1789. From such memorials of her secluded life as have
been printed, one gathers that she had been more or less
of an invalid from quite early years, but that there was
a short period when she could take her part in such social
life as the Evangelical principles of that time allowed.
In 1821 she had a distressing illness from which there
seems to have been no real recovery, though for some
years at least the summers brought enough relief to permit of easy traveling and visits to friends.

In 1822 she fell under the influence of Dr. Cæsar
Malan, a pastor from Geneva, while her spirit was tossed
about with the " fightings and fears within, without "
so natural to her condition and prospects; and under his
ministries of healing her faith took a firmer grip and her
heart found peace. It was well indeed: how else could
she have borne so nobly what was before her, fifty years
of invalidism, with much suffering and frequent periods
of utter prostration and helplessness?

The printed memorials of Miss Elliott deal very
frankly with her spiritual secrets, but do not, so far as

CHARLOTTE ELLIOTT

the writer has observed, disclose the nature of the physical ailment from which she suffered. Hers was the day
when gentle womanhood was veiled in " delicacy," and
doubtless any explanation of her bodily trouble would
have been regarded as indelicate. It does not matter now,
except to students of the reactions of body and spirit.
What matters are those fifty years of patience and even
of service.

It has been objected against Miss Elliott's familiar
hymn, " My God and Father, while I stray," with its refrain, " Thy will be done," that its acceptance of God's
will for our lives is too passive, that it stops with resig-
nation and does not go forward to coöperation. If the
objection is just, and perhaps it is, then the hymn fails
to express her own ideal and practice. For the ideal of
life which this elect lady set up in her heart included
not only a purpose to glorify God by her patience and
pluck but also to make use of such gifts of service as
she had ; especially a literary gift which in girlhood had
expressed itself in humorous verse, but now in religious
poetry and hymns of a very tender and often beautiful
quality.

We do not know how soon she began to exercise her
talent. A number of her hymns appear in a collection
her brother printed in 1835. Her sister says it was a
correspondent, the Rev. Hugh White, who set her the
congenial task of rearranging a little collection of hymns
for the sick room made by a Miss Kiernan, of Dublin,
during her last illness in 1834. To this, published as *The
Invalid's Hymn Book,* Miss Elliott contributed in all
more than a hundred of her own composition. The little
book was warmly welcomed and often reprinted. It was
followed in 1836 by her *Hours of Sorrow,* from a presen-

If Dr Jephson (who cheers so many "hours of sorrow" by his kindness, & alleviates so many sufferings by his skill) will allow this little volume to be sometimes his silent assistant, in the chamber of sickness, & in the house of mourning, he will confer an additional favor on its writer, who has long been, and hopes ever to be his obliged & grateful friend.

C.E.

Westfield Lodge
Dec. 12. 1836.

A NOTE ON THE FLYLEAF OF A COPY OF "HOURS OF SORROW"

tation copy of which the autograph note here reproduced is taken; by *Morning and Evening Hymns for a Week* in 1839; and after a long interval, by *Thoughts in verse on sacred Subjects* in 1869. Her own hours of sorrow ceased at Brighton on September 22, 1871.

She had indeed learned in suffering what she taught in song. All the more welcome, therefore, are the glimpses we catch in her letters of the compensations she herself found in her hymn writing, — the human pleasure of success and the spiritual satisfaction of doing good: " It will be a real delight to me to send you a copy of the *Invalid's Hymn Book*. I have just had a copy bound for dear Queen Adelaide, and shall be much pleased if I find she likes it." And this, a year later: " I have now before me a few supplemental hymns for the third edition of the *Invalid's Hymn Book,* which I have just corrected, and of which the last has sold so quickly. The fifth edition of the *Week's Hymns* is now all sold; and Seeley tells me the *Hours of Sorrow* sell well, so that I feel as if I ought to strive to finish and continue these little works ' which are given me to do.' "

THE "TRUE HISTORY" OF THE HYMN

The annals of a sick room are obscure, and in Miss Elliott's case it is not always easy to get the date of the writing or even of the first publication of a given hymn. It is so with the one before us, of which no manuscript is known to exist. Most books that deal with it repeat the story that connects it with the ministrations of Dr. Malan to Miss Elliott in 1822. They even lay it out on the precise lines of a responsive service. The pastor exhorts the invalid to come to Christ. She answers, " How

can I come? " He tells her, " Come just as you are ";
and she responds, " Just as I am, without one plea." For
the truth of all this there seems to be no evidence whatever, and no amount of repetition adds anything to its
veracity. Truth indeed is a shy bird, and many good
sportsmen fail to bag it.

The Rev. Handley C. G. Moule, afterwards Bishop of
Durham, printed in *The Record* of October 16, 1897, the
" true history " of the hymn, of which he said, " as Miss
Elliott's nephew by marriage I happen to know the precise circumstances of its composition." The bishop
stamps as " inaccurate " the stories that connect the
hymn in any way with her conversion and does not think
she could point to any early crisis of conversion. He al-
ludes to the spiritual comfort Dr. Malan brought her,
and goes on:

" But ill health still beset her . . . it often caused
her the peculiar pain of a seeming uselessness in her life
while the circle round her was full of unresting service-
ableness for God. Such a time of trial marked the year
1834, when she was forty-five years old, and living in
Westfield Lodge, Brighton. . . . Her brother, the Rev.
H. V. Elliott, had not long before conceived the plan of
St. Mary's Hall, at Brighton — a school designed to give,
at nominal cost, a high education to the daughters of
clergymen. . . . In aid of St. Mary's Hall there was to
be held a bazaar. . . . Westfield Lodge was all astir;
every member of the large circle was occupied morning
and night in the preparations, with the one exception of
the ailing sister Charlotte — as full of eager interest as
any of them, but physically fit for nothing. The night
before the bazaar she was kept wakeful by distressing
thoughts of her apparent uselessness; and these thoughts

passed — by a transition easy to imagine — into a spiritual conflict, till she questioned the reality of her whole spiritual life, and wondered whether it were anything better than an illusion of the emotions, an illusion ready to be sorrowfully dissolved.

" The next day, the busy day of the bazaar, she lay upon her sofa. . . . The troubles of the night came back upon her with such force that she felt they must be met and conquered in the grace of God. She gathered up in her soul the great certainties, not of her emotions, but of her salvation: her Lord, his power, his promise. And taking pen and paper from the table she deliberately set down in writing, for her own comfort, ' the formulæ of her faith.' Hers was a heart which always tended to express its depths in verse. So in verse she restated to herself the gospel of pardon, peace, and heaven. ' Probably without difficulty or long pause ' she wrote the hymn. . . .

" As the day wore on, her sister-in-law, Mrs. H. V. Elliott, came in to see her, and bring news of the work. She read the hymn, and asked (she well might) for a copy. So it first stole out from that quiet room into the world."

With this story of the hymn agrees in all particulars an account furnished about 1902 to Mr. Francis A. Jones by " Mrs. Synge, a niece of the authoress." And it is interesting to note that the title-pages of the various editions of Miss Elliott's *Hymns for a Week* bear the inscription: " Sold for the benefit of St. Mary's Hall, Brighton."

Bishop Moule says the hymn was written in 1834, and nobody is in a position to question that date. But the time and place of its first printing are equally interesting, and on these points he is not convincing. He says it appeared in the 1834 edition of *The Invalid's Hymn Book;* and that " in 1835 it was printed, unknown to the writer and without her name, as a leaflet; one of the first copies was given to her by a friend with the words, 'I am sure this will please you.'" Dr. Julian a high authority, writing with the 1834 book before him, says the hymn is not there, and was first printed in the edition of 1836. Dr. Telford, a careful student of Wesleyan hymns, remarks that the hymn was printed a second time in 1836 in Miss Elliott's *Hours of Sorrow;* but it is not found in the writer's copy of that date. Finally, the writer's Canadian friend, James Edmund Jones, Esq., who published a carefully annotated edition of *The Book of Common Praise* in 1909, says there that " Just as I am " is not in *The Invalid's Hymn Book* of 1836, but in the edition of 1841 for the first time. All that the present writer can contribute at first hand to this hotchpotch is to say that the earliest printing of the hymn he has seen with his own eyes is in the 1841 edition of *The Invalid's Hymn Book.*

Whatever may be the exact date of publication, it marks the beginning of a wide circulation, of a wonderful career of usefulness. The Rev. Mr. Elliott (he who founded St. Mary's Hall) thought his sister had done more by a single hymn than he had accomplished " in the course of a long ministry." There is hardly an evangelist without some tale to tell illustrating the power of this hymn. Some such testimonies reached the authoress herself. Probably the one that pleased her most was the grateful letter from the husband of Dora Wordsworth, the " one and matchless daughter " of the great poet. " Now *my* hymn," he reports that sufferer as saying every morning of the last two months of her life; " and she would often and often repeat it after me, line for line, many times in the day and night. I do not think Mr. Wordsworth could bear to have it repeated in his presence, but he is not the less sensible of the solace it gave his one and matchless daughter."

SOME POINTS FOR DISCUSSION

1. It is interesting to find two evangelical-hearted bishops of the Protestant Episcopal Church praising this hymn in practically identical terms as shrining the heart of Christ's gospel. Bishop Stevens of Pennsylvania, writing a preface for an American reprint of *Hymns for a Week,* says of it: " That hymn is the metrical compendium of the Gospel. It is so simple that a child can understand it, so truthful that the heart taught of the Spirit instinctively approves it, so fervent that the soul is warmed into glowing ardor by its burning words, so grand and comprehensive that the departing saint delights to use it as he commits his blood-washed soul into the hands of his faithful Creator." Bishop McIlvaine of Ohio tells us that in 1860 he resumed a custom of gathering the clergy around the chancel, at the close of the annual Convention, for some parting words, a hymn and extempore prayer. " I had chosen [' Just as I am '] to be sung and had it printed on cards; and I have adopted it for all time to come, as long as I shall be here, as *my hymn,* always to be sung on such occasions, and always to the same tune. That hymn contains my religion, my theology, my hope. It has been my ministry to preach just what it contains. In health it expresses all my refuge; in death I desire that I may know noth-

ing else, for support and consolation, but what it contains. When I am gone, I wish to be remembered in
association with that hymn."

In Miss Elliott's books the hymn was printed beneath
the text, " Him that cometh to me I will in no wise cast
out," and it is to be studied in relation to that text. It
may be worth while to make an analysis of the hymn, to
see just what is added verse by verse as to the terms of
the gospel. That done, one would be in a position to
estimate a seventh verse added afterwards by the authoress, as found in the writer's copy of the 1849 edition of
Hours of Sorrow:

> Just as I am — of that free love,
> " The breadth, length, depth, and height " to prove,
> Here for a season, then above —
> O Lamb of God, I come!

2. There are some striking phrases in the hymn. Principal Alexander Whyte, who liked to lecture on it, used
to dwell on the opening *" Just* as I am," as a stroke of
evangelical genius. " A better selected word is not in
all the world." But why? He also contrasted the coming for " healing of the mind " with Macbeth's " Canst
thou not minister to a mind diseas'd? " (Act v,
scene iii).

The line,

> " Fightings and fears within, without,"

has a parallel in a good many other hymns. We have
noted:

Wars without, and Fights within. John Cennick, 1741.
Fightings without, and fears within. John Newton, 1779,
By war without, and fears within. John Newton, 1779.
Foes without and fears within. J. D. Burns, 1857.
Fightings without, and fears each day within. H. Bonar, 1879.

Are these writers quoting from one another, or is there some text of Scripture appropriated by each in turn?

3. Of the two tunes to these words in *The Hymnal revised,* Bradbury's appeared in *The Mendelssohn Collection* of tunes, edited by Thomas Hastings and himself in 1849. Bradbury was a pupil of Lowell Mason, and his tunes mark the transition from Mason's simple but dignified music to the livelier " gospel hymns " that followed. He " won boundless popularity for light tunes in the Sunday schools." Few of his church tunes survive.

Familiar as is the association of his "Woodworth " with " Just as I am," many will think such words worthy of a better tune. Whether Sir Joseph Barnby has furnished it in his setting is open to debate. He was a much more accomplished musician than Bradbury, with a lovely gift for melody, and greatly under the influence of Gounod. Many of his tunes are in the four-part-song style and seemed effeminate to lovers of solid old Psalm tunes.

The number of good tunes adapted to the peculiar meter of " Just as I am " is rather limited; but a repetition of the final " I come " transfers the hymn to the long-meter class, and once there, the choice of tunes becomes almost boundless.

XVIII

I HEARD THE VOICE OF JESUS SAY

THE TEXT OF THE HYMN

1   I heard the voice of Jesus say,
     " Come unto Me and rest;
   Lay down, thou weary one, lay down
     Thy head upon My breast."
   I came to Jesus as I was,
     Weary and worn and sad,
   I found in Him a resting-place,
     And He has made me glad.

2   I heard the voice of Jesus say,
     " Behold, I freely give
   The living water; thirsty one,
     Stoop down and drink, and live."
   I came to Jesus, and I drank
     Of that life-giving stream;
   My thirst was quenched, my soul revived,
     And now I live in Him.

3   I heard the voice of Jesus say,
     " I am this dark world's Light;
   Look unto Me, thy morn shall rise,
     And all thy day be bright."
   I looked to Jesus, and I found
     In Him my Star, my Sun;
   And in that light of life I'll walk,
     Till traveling days are done.

Rev. Horatius Bonar, 1846

NOTE: The text is taken from *Hymns of Faith and Hope* (the first series), where it bears the title, " The Voice from Galilee." The quotation marks indicating the words of Christ are not given there, and for " quenched " the reading is " quench'd."

One sunny morning in the summer of 1887 the writer was making a call upon the Rev. Dr. William G. Blaikie at his home in the city of Edinburgh. In the course of it Dr. Blaikie drew him to the front window, and, point-

HORATIUS BONAR

ing to a figure on the opposite pavement, said, " That is Horatius Bonar "; adding, " I thought you would like to see him," or some words to that effect. It was indeed a group rather than a figure to which Dr. Blaikie pointed. In the center was a venerable man in clerical black, bowed down with years and tottering in infirmity, with an arm thrown across the shoulders of an attendant on either side, who had apparently no easy task to keep him upon his feet. And this central figure, with the large frame and head, and the white hair and whiskers around the fresh skin of the face, having even in extreme weakness that look of nobility which seems the peculiar characteristic of the Scottish type of old age — this venerable figure was Horatius Bonar, the author of " I heard the voice of Jesus say," and of many another hymn familiar in our churches.

THE GREATEST OF SCOTTISH HYMN WRITERS

When one recalls the fact that his hymn, " I lay my sins on Jesus," was written before 1837, what could be less surprising than finding the Bonar of 1887 venerable and broken? He was then in the last years of a long life. His latest appearance in public was in the following April, although he lingered here until the thirty-first of July, 1889. Born December 19, 1808, in Edinburgh, where his father was second solicitor of Excise and a ruling elder of the Church of Scotland, the outward course of his life was peculiarly quiet and uneventful. Its one striking event was his secession from the established Church of Scotland. He had finished his studies at the University of Edinburgh, had gone into the ministry, and been ordained as minister of the North Parish in the border town of Kelso. Just then there was a good deal of unrest throughout the Church, caused by the action of " patrons " who held as their property the right of naming the parish minister, and only too often put in their nominee against the vehement protest of the congregation. This led to the great Disruption of 1843, and Bonar with many of his friends was among the four hundred and fifty-one ministers who withdrew from the Establishment and formed " the Free Church of Scotland."

Most controversies are capable of being adjusted in time and schism is never lovely. But these men were conscientious and many of them were heroic in thus renouncing their only means of support. Mr. Bonar and his parish were exceptional in being able to retain their property, and he continued at Kelso as the devoted pastor of the church, now " Free," until 1866.

Some have wondered that one so gifted should spend the greater part of his ministry in the obscure country-side. Invitations to go elsewhere were not wanting. But he was absorbed in his pastoral work and in evangelistic labors which took in the whole Border country. " Here I am, and here I must remain till my Lord come to me or for me," he wrote to a church at Newcastle; and he heard no clear call until, in 1866, the opportunity came to found a new church in his native city. He was a man set apart. He hated publicity and counted recognition and honors from men's hands a very empty thing. He was like a pilgrim and stranger on the earth, anxious to make it better for his passing through, but homesick for heaven. He lived with God, the humblest of His children, and had only one great aim in his life — to bring men to Christ.

Those quiet years at Kelso no doubt made him what he was intellectually and spiritually. There he carried on his studies and attained the culture that is more than scholarship. But, as in all he did, even his studies centered in Christ. His attention was turned to the interpretation of prophecy and he became an ardent "premillenarian." He believed that our Lord was to return in person, soon, suddenly, and with power; to destroy antichrist and restore Israel, and to inaugurate an earthly kingdom of a thousand years. The Advent hope became an absorbing passion. In its light he lived and worked, and to spread it he wrote tracts and books, and for twenty-five years edited *The Quarterly Journal of Prophecy.*

This sense of detachment from the present world, this homesickness for heaven, this hopeful but pensive expectation of the Second Coming, are behind his hymns and make them what they are. " There is nobody like Bonar to sing about heaven," exclaims one of the characters in Miss Phelps's *Gates Ajar.* And it is true: nobody since the time of Bernard of Cluny. His hymns are like those that came out of the seclusion and otherworldliness of the medieval monasteries, where the monks sang of the growing evil of the world outside, of the absent Bridegroom, and of the glories of Jerusalem the golden. "What! " said a High Church lady at Torquay, on meeting a member of Bonar's Edinburgh congregation: " Is Bonar, the hymn writer, still alive? I always understood he was a medieval saint."

He was in his fifty-seventh year when he went to Edinburgh to spend the remainder of life in upbuilding a new parish. Largely under Dr. Thomas Chalmers' influence he had entered the ministry; under Chalmers' leadership he had exchanged the established Church for the Free; and in his regard that leader persisted as " the greatest man he had ever met." He found special pleasure therefore in becoming first pastor of the Chalmers Memorial Church. In Edinburgh, as in the Border, he was evangelist as well as pastor, and when Dwight L. Moody came to Scotland, Bonar took an active part in his mission and even wrote some hymns for Sankey. Sankey had set to music Tennyson's song from " Guinevere," " Late, late, so late! and dark the night and chill! " And, when copyright difficulties prevented its printing, Bonar furnished a substitute, " ' Yet there is room ': the Lamb's bright hall of song."

In 1883 Dr. Bonar was made Moderator of the Free Church Assembly. The photograph of him here reproduced showed (more clearly than a reproduction can) the facings on the coat of the court dress prescribed by custom for a moderator's wear. His last sermon in the Chalmers Memorial was preached on September 11, 1887.

At his funeral his assistant, the Rev. J. M. Sloan, drove to the Canongate churchyard in the same carriage with Principal Cairns and Dr. Cuyler of Brooklyn. The three men fell to discussing their preferences among Bonar's hymns. One spoke for " Here, O my Lord, I see Thee face to face "; another, for " When the weary, seeking rest "; the third, for " I heard the voice of Jesus say."

THE STORY OF THE HYMN

It was the shortest of stories according to Dr. Bonar. " I have nothing on record but a little scrap of paper without a date and the hymn written in pencil." But, thanks to his son, we can now do a little better than that.

For the year before his ordination Bonar was assistant at St. John's, Leith, and superintended the Sunday school. He worried because the children took no interest in the singing. Nothing was provided for them except the Scottish Psalms in meter and a few hymns set to solemn tunes, and neither the words nor music appealed to them. The young superintendent tried the experiment of writing simpler hymns to melodies the scholars already knew. " I lay my sins on Jesus " set to " Heber " and " The morning, the bright and the beautiful morning " set to " The Flowers of the Forest," were the first, printed on little leaflets. The results were so happy that he wrote a few more, including " I was a wandering sheep," and printed them with a number of selected hymns on new leaflets.

Evidently the ban against human hymns was not strictly enforced in the home and Sunday school, but there was as yet no movement to introduce them into the church service. When the Free Church went out in 1843 it kept on using the metrical Psalms as a matter of course, and during the whole of Bonar's ministry at Kelso, no hymns were sung in his church other than the group of Paraphrases already in the Psalm books.

His first hymn for grown people, " Go, labor on," was written at Leith, to hearten his fellow workers in his mission district. After he went to the quieter scenes of Kelso, his hymn writing grew into a habit. He kept a note book at his side or in his pocket, wherever he went, in which he would jot down a thought or a line or a verse, to be worked up at leisure, or even a hymn hastily written in pencil, with contractions, elisions, and sometimes a phrase in shorthand.

Dr. Bonar's son has had some pages from these notebooks reproduced, and we have before us a rough draft of " I heard the voice of Jesus say." Here, indeed, is the story of the hymn as we see it unfolding like a flower from the first seed thought to the perfect form.

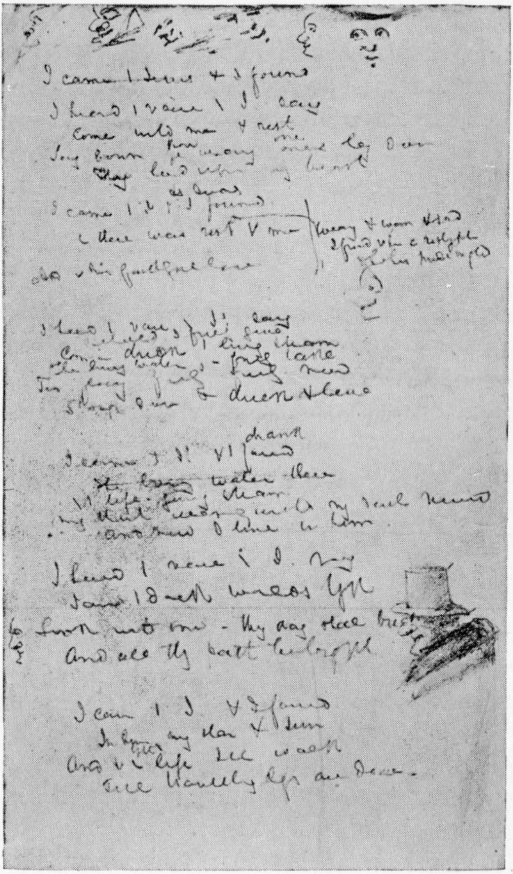

THE ROUGH DRAFT OF THE HYMN

We have even the quaint little designs in the margin that the hand makes almost unconsciously while the brain is shaping its thoughts. The reproduction is somewhat faint, but the original was in pencil and is now rubbed and faded. The photographer who copied it is said to have required an exposure of three quarters of an hour to get the result that we have before us.

In the notebook this hymn comes next to the well-known Advent hymn, " The Church has waited long." It is not printed among the seventeen of his own hymns Dr. Bonar included in his *The Bible Hymn Book* of 1845, and is said to have appeared first in another collection, *Hymns original and selected*, 1846, which the present writer has not seen. As one after another notebook filled up during those quiet years at Kelso, Dr. Bonar gathered and printed his hymns as *Hymns of Faith and Hope;* a first volume in 1857, a second in 1861, a third in 1866. After going to Edinburgh he brought out three more volumes: *The Song of the new Creation* in 1872, *Hymns of the Nativity* in 1879, and *Communion Hymns* in 1881.

When these " Hymns of Faith and Hope " were new they took the religious world by storm. They were so fresh and original, so beautiful in phrase and melodious, so spiritual and tender, that people were disposed to make a cult of them and to say, " There never were such hymns as these." Canon Duncan, speaking no doubt for England rather than for Bonar's Scotland, is responsible for the statement that " they were at one time found in almost every Christian home." And the editors of hymn books vied with one another in putting a representative selection of them before the congregations.

Well, novelty wears off and an indiscriminate popularity always brings about a reaction of criticism if not
indifference. Moreover the atmosphere of the religious
world changes, whether for better or worse, and at
present Bonar's thought of life as a pilgrimage and his
homesickness for heaven do not make the wide appeal
they once did. These changing conditions have affected
the popularity of his hymns. The critics say now that
some of them are careless and some repetitious and me-
chanical; and good people say that others of them are
somewhat morbid. And so it has come about that fewer
of Bonar's hymns are sung today than was the case a
generation ago. One can feel some sympathy, perhaps,
with a present-day bustling Christian who says that " A
few more years shall roll " gets on his nerves; but it is
hard to belive that any changes of atmosphere will affect
" I heard the voice of Jesus say." It adds something
even to the beautiful words of Christ: it adds the human
response, without which Christ's words were quite in
vain.

SOME POINTS FOR DISCUSSION

1. This hymn captivates us by its lyrical beauty, but
it deserves careful study. Bishop Fraser, of Manchester,
England, regarded it as the best in the language. It
belongs to the class known as " subjective hymns " or
" hymns of inward experience." Like so many of
Bonar's, it mirrors the life of Christ in the soul. If the
writer understands it, it pictures human life as a pilgrimage (Bonar seems to have thought of life in no other
aspect). The pilgrim has sought far and wide for things
unattained. As night comes on he is weary of it all, he
hears " The Voice from Galilee," and heeding it finds

rest. But the new peace in the heart must be sustained, and the pilgrim reaches out his hand to take from Christ's the offered water of life. And thus refreshed he rests in the Lord. At dawn he awakes, at peace but a pilgrim still. It is another day and he must go on — but not to resume the old quest. It is a new day of which Christ is the Light, and a transfigured world through which Christ is the Way. And in that Light and by that Way he will walk " till traveling days are done."

Is this a fair interpretation of the hymn?

2. Some of us will recall a discussion of the comparative merits of Dickens and Thackeray as novelists, in which the after-dinner speaker, having laid out his approaches in cold blood, waxes warmer and warmer as he proceeds, until he ends in a spluttering confusion of cross currents through which all that the ear can catch are excited references to Dackeray and Thickens or Thickeray and Dackens.

The purpose of this little skit no doubt was to poke fun at criticism by comparison, the method of appraising one writer by contrasting him with another. But the method has its use, if only for bringing out the distinctive features of each writer. It is not unprofitable, for instance, to ask how the hymns of Bonar stand comparison with those of Watts and Charles Wesley. We might start by comparing what is regarded as the best hymn of each writer: Watts's "When I survey the wondrous cross," Wesley's "Jesus, Lover of my soul," and Bonar's " I heard the voice of Jesus say."

The comparison may well be confined to Bonar's choicer hymns. As was the case both with Watts and Wesley, he wrote far too much, and allowed facility to usurp the place of inspiration. Like them he was at times an extremely careless workman, and for some reason never corrected infelicities that a little thought might have remedied. In all the editions of his *Hymns of Faith and Hope,* so far as the writer has collated them, the plates remain unaltered, even as to a printer's slip. Bonar had also a painful way of ringing the changes on his thought to wearisome lengths, through a series of lines and phrases repeated with modifications of some of their words, after the manner of Southey in his " Cataract of Lodore." " Beyond the smiling and the weeping " is his best in this manner. But even the poorest of the hymns *are by Bonar:* they share in an individuality of thought and expression which is as fresh and characteristic as Charles Wesley's was.

3. How are we to trace Bonar's lineage and assign him his place in the development of hymn writing as we have followed it in these studies? He was, to begin with, a Scottish hymn writer with few predecessors. And is there anything in Watts or Wesley to suggest him as a pupil in the school of either? He was more akin to the writers of the Evangelical Revival, but his own Evangelical theology he took not from them but directly from the stern Reformation standards of Scotland, and drew forth crystal streams from that massive rock. He seems like a prophet, solitary and apart from the line of priestly succession.

4. The correspondents' column in one of the literary weeklies had a query, " Is it true that no Presbyterian writers have contributed hymns of lasting position to the general stores of the Church? " There had been a discussion on the subject perhaps, and some Presbyterian was out looking for ammunition with which to defend the claims of his own denomination.

Most people would now agree that the question is not very important. We choose our hymns for what they are, without anxiety as to the church connection of their authors. The modern hymn book presents the nearest approach to church unity so far achieved. If, however, the question is raised, it is answered by saying that Bonar's hymns are sung in all Churches and are the chief Presbyterian contribution to the common stock. Among other Presbyterian hymn writers appearing in the index of authors in *The Hymnal revised* are:

(1) From Scotland: Bruce, Logan, Morison, J. D. Burns, Norman MacLeod, Matheson, Miss Borthwick and Mrs. Findlater, Brownlie, Mrs. Cousin, and the Duke of Argyll.

(2) From Canada: Robert Murray.

(3) From the United States: Davies, J. W. Alexander, Duffield, Dunn, Hastings, Mrs. Prentiss, Wolfe, Hopper, March, Mrs. C. L. Smith, and van Dyke.

XIX

THERE IS A GREEN HILL FAR AWAY

THE TEXT OF THE HYMN

1 There is a green hill far away,
   Without a city wall,
  Where the dear Lord was crucified,
   Who died to save us all.

2 We may not know, we cannot tell,
   What pains He had to bear;
  But we believe it was for us
   He hung and suffered there.

3 He died that we might be forgiven,
   He died to make us good,
  That we might go at last to heaven,
   Saved by His precious blood.

4 There was no other good enough
   To pay the price of sin;
  He only could unlock the gate
   Of heaven, and let us in.

5 O dearly, dearly has He loved,
   And we must love Him too,
  And trust in His redeeming blood,
   And try His works to do.

Cecil Frances Humphreys (afterwards Mrs. Alexander), 1848

NOTE: The text is taken from the third edition of *Hymns for little Children*, in which the second line is relieved from what was apparently a typographical error in the first edition.

HIGH CHURCH HYMNS

This hymn was written by a young Irish lady, Miss Cecil Frances Humphreys, a little before 1848. If the Evangelical authoress of "Just as I am, without one plea" read it, as probably she did, she may have thought it newfangled and queer, but she could not have found anything in it contrary to the doctrines she loved. And yet she must have disapproved very strongly of its writer, for that lady was one of the young people brought up on the Evangelical side of the Church who had come under the influence of the new High Church Movement and adopted the very "Puseyite errors" against which Miss Elliott kept warning her friends.

To understand just what that means, we have to re-call a bit of church history. Not long before, in the early eighteen-thirties, the Church of England and of Ireland (disposed at the time to be somewhat drowsy) had been startled by strange goings-on at Oxford Uni-versity, just where the Methodist Movement had started a century before. It was the beginning of what is gen-erally called the Oxford or High Church Movement, of which Newman and Keble and Pusey were among the leaders. To explain its purpose in a sentence is not easy. It aimed to make the Church less Protestant, to bring it closer to the principles of Catholicism — Apostolic Succession, the priesthood of ministers, " high " doctrines of the validity of sacraments, and Catholic ceremonial. Newman and some of the other leaders were to follow out these principles so far as to land themselves in the Roman Catholic Church. But they left behind them in the Church of England a powerful High Church

MRS. ALEXANDER

Party which has grown until it is to-day stronger and more " Catholic " than it ever was.

Now every deeply felt religious movement shows an impulse to make its own songs. The Reformation Movement under Luther filled Germany with hymn singing, and under Calvin turned the Bible Psalms into people's songs. The Methodist movement put its gospel into revival hymns. The Evangelical Movement brought out a wealth of hymns of personal experience. And the High Church Movement has developed a whole com- pany of writers of what we might call " churchly " hymns. A feature of the new movement was its strict observance of fasts, festivals and saints' days, and its setting up of daily services and at least weekly com- munions. Suitable hymns had to be provided for all these occasions, so that many of the new hymns were " churchly " in the narrower sense. Others are churchly only in the broader sense in which all good Christians love the Church and the sanctities of God's House. And there are of course many more which deal with those experiences of the gospel that lie deeper in the heart than any theories of the Church that divide us.

To say that the High Church Movement has inspired a large proportion of the best hymns of the nineteenth century is simply to acknowledge the truth. And so it happens that as we go forward in these studies we shall have to follow the footsteps of Miss Humphreys and cross over from the Evangelical side to the High Church side of the Church of England, if we are to find some of the hymns most familiar and best loved. In making the crossing it may be as well to acknowledge that a disregard of the claims of aesthetic feeling has always been a weaker side of the Evangelical Movement.

WHY THE HYMN WAS WRITTEN

" There is a green hill far away " is not a High Church hymn nor even a churchly hymn, so far as its contents go. It might have been written by an Evangelical; and in fact Miss Humphreys never gave up her Evangelical beliefs. Nevertheless the hymn was inspired by her new churchly ideals and written as a part of a plan to extend them.

She felt that if the Catholic principles of the Oxford Movement were to prevail, a beginning must be made by instilling " sound Church principles " into the children. And a first step was to provide them with attractive hymns setting forth those principles. She wrote some and tried them on her Sunday-school class. When she had written forty she published them in 1848 as *Hymns for little Children*, seventy-two pages in all. There were two daily hymns, one on the Holy Trinity, a group expounding the Order in the Prayer Book for a child's baptism, and other groups on the Apostles' Creed, the Commandments and the Lord's Prayer: her selection of topics being evidently intended to cover just the things a child was expected to know at its confirmation.

" There is a green hill far away " was one of the Apostles' Creed group, set beneath the article, " Suffered under Pontius Pilate, was crucified, dead, and buried." Now it is necessary to know this original setting of the hymn, the where and the why of its printing, in order to understand it. Some people have failed to understand it and have misjudged it. Dr. Theodore L. Cuyler, a great lover of hymns and not a bad judge of them, wrote to *The New York Evangelist* in 1895: " I

The Palace,
Derry.

18ᵗʰ Decᵇ 1883

O. for the pearly gates of Heaven
O for the golden floor
O. for the Sun of Righteousness
That setteth nevermore.

Cecil Frances Alexander

AN AUTOGRAPHED VERSE FROM MRS. ALEXANDER'S PEN

confess that this popular lyric has always seemed to me more like a snatch of sacred geography and sound theology than a burst of praise." Some theologians on the other hand have objected that the " theology " was too vague, and that " He died to make us good " is not an intelligent statement of the atonement.

These objections are covered by knowing that it is a child's hymn, picturesque because a child takes in a picture more readily than a thought, and endeavoring to state doctrine from a child's point of view and in a child's language. Its whole beauty lies in its simplicity, and if it should tempt the most systematic theologian to share even for a moment the mind of a child that would be an added grace.

A number of Miss Humphreys' hymns have taken their place among the classics of Christian childhood. But this hymn has gone further than that. It has firmly established itself as a standard church hymn. There is a type of children's literature, such as *Alice in Wonderland* and Kenneth Grahame's *The Golden Age,* that appeals irresistibly to the child within us all; and the best of Miss Humphreys' children's hymns are of that type. Her " There is a green hill far away," like Phillips Brooks's " O little town of Bethlehem," cannot be hidden in the nursery or confined within the Sunday schoolroom.

THE AUTHOR OF THE HYMN

It is usually spoken of as written by Mrs. Alexander, wife of the Irish bishop or archbishop of that name, just as " Lead, kindly Light " is spoken of as the work of Cardinal Newman. But Newman was a Protestant clergyman when he wrote his hymn, and Cecil Humphreys was not yet married when she wrote this one: when she did marry, her husband was not a bishop but rector of a remote parish, and did not become arch-bishop until after her death.

Miss Humphreys was the daughter of a major in the Royal Marines, a Norfolk gentleman who as a land owner and land agent had come to reside in Wicklow County, Ireland. She was born there in 1818 and spent all her life in Ireland.

She wrote verses as a child, and it is not clear just how she was turned from the Evangelical wing of the Church to the High Church side. The romantic features of the Oxford Movement would appeal to her, and no doubt the beautiful poetry of John Keble's *Christian Year* helped. Her first volume of poetry, *Verses for holy Seasons,* was itself a " Christian Year " adapted to the capacities of children. It had a hymn for every Sunday and every other day provided for in the Prayer Book " in a kind of sing-song style of versification " a child could easily learn. That was in 1846. Her *Hymns for little Children* followed two years later, and had a preface by John Keble.

In October, 1850, she married the Rev. William Alex-ander, a rector in Tyrone, and a very eloquent preacher, who seventeen years later became Bishop of Derry and Raphoe and ultimately " Primate of all Ireland." She was admirably fitted to be a pastor's wife. She was as far as possible from the dreamy, ineffectual type of poet. She never posed, detested gush and sentimentality, had a direct tongue and incisive speech, and she turned a vigilant eye upon her husband's house, garden and farm. She kept her devotional life largely hidden in her heart, but was a strict " Prayer Book Christian," going to church every day and to communion every week. Beyond that her days were largely given over to errands of charity and helpfulness, from one poor Irish home to another, from one sick-bed to another, from one house of sorrow to another, no matter how remote. She knew all her neighbors, and loved them, especially the Irish Presbyterians. " Dear, good people! " she would say; " how kind they are to me, how ready to give for Christ's sake! I *do* like them."

When her husband became bishop in 1867, she was brought more into contact with society and large institutions. She became the hostess of many distinguished people and shared the publicity of a bishop's life. But she was as much at home in the back streets of Londonderry as in the Bishop's Palace. It was in the palace she died on October 12, 1895, and to her funeral a great throng gathered from England as well as from Ireland, thus paying a spontaneous tribute to a noble life.

If some of them were paying tribute also to the very real vein of poetry that was in her, she herself would not have welcomed it. She was possibly the only poet that ever lived who did not like to hear her poems praised. " Again and again," her husband says, " I have read to her words of lofty, of almost impassioned commendation from men of genius or holiness, of rank and position. She listened without a remark and looked up almost with a frown." The exception was his reading a little tract by an English nonconformist minister. It told the story (for whose truth the writer vouched) of a great change in the heart and life of a very worldly man. He happened to hear " There is a green hill far away " exquisitely sung. It awakened feelings and yearnings that proved to be the starting point of a new life. " Mrs. Alexander almost sprang from her chair, looked me in the face, and said: ' Thank God! I do like to hear *that*.' "

SOME POINTS FOR DISCUSSION

1. The second line of this hymn has an interesting little history all its own.

When *Hymns for little Children* was printed in 1848 it read there:

> " Beside a ruined city wall."

That must have been a blunder, one would think, because the two extra syllables could not possibly be sung to a common meter tune. In the third edition (1849), the line reads,

> " Without a city wall,"

and so it still stands in the 234th thousand issue of 1864.

But sometime later the authoress was asked by a small child what was meant by a green hill not having a city wall; and so she changed the dubious " without " to " outside," and in her latest text and in *Hymns ancient and modern* the line reads,

> " Outside a city wall."

And yet when Bishop Alexander published her *Poems* after her death, he restored the " without," which certainly falls more pleasantly on the ear. Is there any real necessity for resorting to " outside "?

2. Nothing sounds more sweet to us than the hymns we love sung by the lips of children. But when we ask what impression the words they sing make upon the

children's own hearts and minds, we get a different point
of view altogether. The line we have just discussed il-
lustrates the difficulty of getting to a child's mind.
There are other illustrations in plenty. The child who
asked for the hymn about " the boy who stole the
watch " was referring to

> " The old man, meek and mild,
>   The priest of Israel, slept;
> His *watch* the temple-child,
>   The little Levite, *kept.*"

Dr. Watts was the first Englishman to write hymns children could understand: they could hardly mistake

> " Let dogs delight to bark and bite,
>   For God hath made them so; "

and his *Divine Songs for the use of Children* monopo-
lized the field for a century. Charles Wesley tried to
improve upon them with his *Hymns for Children*. Of
these Dr. A. E. Gregory, not the less a good Wesleyan
for his sense of humor, remarks that some of them must
have frightened a poor little Methodist out of his wits.
And the Taylor sisters, Ann and Jane, followed in 1810
with their *Hymns for infant minds,* almost too infantile,
it seems now, but widely used in their day.

When the High Church Movement began there were
no children's hymns extant that fitted in with High
Church ideals. Miss Humphreys was only one of several who tried to provide them, but she was the most
successful with her *Hymns for little Children*. And yet
even of these the proportion that won their way was
small, and of the children's hymns of her later life, which
were very many, scarcely any are even remembered.

If then it is so extremely difficult to write good children's hymns, and if children get the strangest notions out of their hymns even when they are good, a question opens out that is at least worthy of discussion. May it not prove the wise course to encourage the children to learn the great hymns of the Church while memory is strong, with such explanations as we can give, trusting that as they grow older the hymns securely lodged in their memory will prove a life-long treasure? Is not this the course we pursue in respect of the Bible, the Creed, and the Commandments, much of which is beyond a child's understanding?

3. This hymn had the honor of being set to music, as a solo, by one of the most distinguished of modern French musicians, Charles François Gounod, who is said to have remarked that the words themselves were so musical they hardly needed such setting. His music to the minds of many is the most perfect interpretation of the hymn. Mr. Gower's " Meditation," to which the words are set in *The Hymnal revised,* was written for " There is a land of pure delight," but is becoming more and more closely attached to the present hymn. Mr. Gower was an Englishman who came early to this country, engaging himself with mining interests at Denver, Colorado, where he died in 1922. The tune " Horsley," printed beneath the words, is the favorite in most English churches, and one of solid worth, likely to grow in the esteem of those who make use of it.

XX

ART THOU WEARY, ART THOU LANGUID

THE TEXT OF THE HYMN

1   Art thou weary, art thou languid,
      Art thou sore distrest?
    " Come to Me," saith One, " and, coming,
      Be at rest."

2   Hath He marks to lead me to Him,
      If He be my Guide?
    " In His feet and hands are wound-prints,
      And his side."

3   Is there diadem, as Monarch,
      That His brow adorns?
    " Yea, a crown, in very surety,
      But of thorns."

4   If I find Him, if I follow,
      What His guerdon here?
    " Many a sorrow, many a labor,
      Many a tear."

5   If I still hold closely to Him,
      What hath He at last?
    " Sorrow vanquished, labor ended,
      Jordan passed."

6   If I ask Him to receive me,
      Will He say me nay?
    " Not till earth and not till heaven
      Pass away."

7 Finding, following, keeping, struggling,
    Is He sure to bless?
  "Saints, apostles, prophets, martyrs,
    Answer, 'Yes.'"

Rev. John Mason Neale, 1862

NOTE: The text is that of Dr. Neale's *Hymns of the Eastern Church translated,* except in the third line of the last verse, which there reads, " Angels, Martyrs, Prophets, Virgins."

A HYMN IN DIALOGUE

The hymn takes the form of a dialogue between an evangelist who offers Christ as the Way to rest and a pilgrim who asks about the signposts and the road. The form is striking but it is not strange. " Watchman, tell us of the night " is also a dialogue, and those who have followed these studies will recall John Cennick and his Sacred Hymns " mostly composed in DIALOGUES."

The conversational form is older still. The Twenty-fourth Psalm is a hymn in dialogue between two choirs, one stationed within the holy walls, the other gathered outside the gate and claiming the right to enter. But in the present hymn the give-and-take between the speakers is brisker, more dramatic.

Its dramatic quality is brought out in a passage toward the close of Sally Pratt McLean's novel, *Cape Cod Folks.* The young men of the village had stayed " down to shore " in the late afternoon putting the finishing touches on " mendin' up the old schooner." In the evening a few sorrowing neighbors gathered at Grandma Keeler's, where Captain Satchell* was telling how George Olver and Lute Cradlebow had sung this hymn together as they worked upon the schooner, just be-

* These names were changed in later editions of the novel.

fore the black squall came, in which Lute went down to his heroic death.

" By and by, *him* and George Olver struck up a song. I've heern 'em sing it before, them two. As nigh as I calk'late, it's about findin' rest in Jesus, and one a askin' questions, all fa'r and squar', to know the way and whether it's a goin' to lead thar' straight or not, and the other answerin'. And *he* — he was a tinkerin,' 'way up on the foremast, George Olver and the rest on us was astern, — and I'll hear to my dyin' day how his voice came a floatin' down to us thar', — chantin'-like it was — cl'ar and fearless and slow. So he asks, for findin' Jesus, ef thar's any marks to foller by ; and George Olver, he answers about them bleedin' nail-prints, and the great one in His side.

" So then that voice comes down ag'in, askin' if thar's any crown, like other kings, to tell Him by ; and George Olver, he answers straight about that crown o' thorns.

" Then says that other voice, floatin' so strong and cl'ar, and if he gin up all and follered, what should he have? what now? So George Olver, he sings deep o' the trial and the sorrowin'. But that other voice never shook, a askin', and what if he helt to Him to the end, what then should it be, what then? George Olver answers : ' Forevermore, the sorrowin' ended — Death gone over.'

" Then he sings out, like his mind was all made up, ' And if he undertook it, would he likely be turned away ? '

" ' And it's likelier,' George Olver answers him, ' that heaven and earth shall pass.'

" So I'll hear it to my dyin' day — his voice a floatin' down to me from up above thar' somewhar', askin' them questions that nobody could ever answer like, so soon, he answered 'em for himself."

THE AUTHOR OF THE HYMN

John Mason Neale was another young recruit of the High Church Party in the Church of England who came over from the Evangelical side. He was born in London in January, 1818; the son of an Evangelical clergyman, and at eighteen was sent up to Cambridge University. The High Church Movement, begun at Oxford, was very active there by this time, and Neale gave himself up to it with his whole heart, becoming as much of a " Catholic " as one can without submitting to the Pope's authority. The spread of the Movement was creating general alarm throughout the country, and Neale, who was nothing if not outspoken, was already a marked man. The Bishop of Winchester refused his license, but Bishop Monk ordained him in 1842. He passed his whole ministry under the shadow of reproach and disfavor. The only preferment in the Church that came to him was the wardenship of Sackville College at East Grinstead, some twenty-nine miles from London. With a high-sounding name the college was merely an endowed alms-house, and the wardenship carried a salary of less than thirty pounds. This position Neale obtained in 1846 and retained until his death there in August, 1866; a period of twenty years, for sixteen of which he was prohibited by his bishop from exercising any ministerial functions, and during several of them was occasionally subject to visitation by the " No-Popery " men.

When he founded at East Grinstead a nursing " Sisterhood of S. Margaret " he was felt to have capped his offenses by adding " a Romish convent " to the resources of a Protestant Church. So intense were the feelings aroused that, when Neale and the Sisters took the body of one who had died to Lewes for burial, they were attacked in the churchyard by a mob. Neale was knocked down and maltreated, the Sisters were hustled along the streets, and the whole party rescued with great difficulty by the police and finally got on board the train for East Grinstead. For such are the reversals of religious history. In one century a man is mobbed for trying to stir up an " Evangelical Revival," in the next for trying to stir up a " Catholic Revival."

Such experiences did not suggest to Neale any compromise of his church views. Those were fixed ideas, on which his whole life was built. He believed that in the " Catholic " system of religion he had found ultimate truth and was incapable of "liberal" views in theology or politics. The opposition or enmity he aroused he met by ignoring it and turning his back upon his accusers. With an elevation of mind that refused to harbor resentment, he calmly pursued his own ideals of life, in which scholarship and charity happily mingled. In his study at East Grinstead or abroad he carried forward his researches on the sources of early church history and worship, bringing forth work after work marked by a learning that in his own lines had no equal and by a productiveness almost without parallel. He gave special attention to the hymns of the Latin Church, to which the minds of High Churchmen had turned as more ancient and seemly than the current hymns of the Evangelicals. He explored their sources, gathered many hitherto unknown, wrote their history, and translated some of them with brilliant success.

DR. JOHN MASON NEALE

But Neale was more than a scholar. He wrote many books for the people, — sermons, young people's stories, " readings " to the aged and the sick. There are some who regard him as a great master of English, and a great teacher of that pure religion which lies deeper than the clash of rival systems. That accomplished bookman, Sir William Robertson Nicoll, himself a Congregationalist and Evangelical, shortly before his death confessed that " Neale's *Readings to the Aged* is my favorite amongst all religious books, and many pages of it I could almost repeat by heart." Good as these books are, it is not by them that Neale's memory is kept green so much as by such hymns as " Jerusalem the golden " and " Art thou weary, art thou languid."

WHY THE HYMN IS CALLED A GREEK HYMN

The Eastern or Greek Church, as well as the Roman, claims to be " Catholic." It claims also to be, like its Lord, unchangeable. And while Newman and others were turning toward the Church of Rome, Neale was strongly disposed to seek a refuge from modern liberalism in that immovable fortress of the faith, the Greek Church. He devoted much time to studying its history and liturgies. He was the first Englishman to tackle what he called "the eighteen quarto books of Greek Church poetry," and in 1862 he published a little volume of *Hymns of the Eastern Church translated.*

It was a wonderful little book: as if he had discovered a forgotten country, not in Arctic regions but in the fertile East, which he had been cultivating alone for twelve years, and now brought into our Western Churches some of the flowers he had raised. Among them were such hymns as " The day is past and over," " Christian, dost thou see them," " The day of resurrection," and " Art thou weary, art thou languid."

A HYMN IN DR. NEALE'S AUTOGRAPH

The book found a ready welcome among those interested in the old church hymns. Only a year earlier a group of clergymen had put forth a collection with the taking title, *Hymns ancient and modern.* It was enthusiastically received by High Churchmen, resented by

Evangelicals, and soon became (as it continues to be) the chief hymnal of the Church of England. By 1868 the time had come to enlarge it, and an " Appendix " of that year afforded the opportunity of adding eight of Neale's hymns of the Eastern Church. Of the eight " Art thou weary " made the quickest appeal to the public: it was simple and touching, and the catchy tune, " Stephanos," has carried it all over the English-speaking world.

It must be acknowledged that the little voyager sailed under false colors. Dr. Neale had launched it flying the Greek flag, and everywhere it was welcomed as an ancient Greek hymn, while in fact it was not a Greek hymn at all, but a modern English hymn composed by Dr. Neale himself.

He had printed it in 1862 among his translations of the *Hymns of the Eastern Church,* naming " S. Stephen the Sabaite," an eighth century Syrian monk, as its author, giving a sketch of his life, quoting the first line of the hymn in Greek, even naming the particular service book in which he had found it: " I copy," he said, " from a dateless Constantinopolitan book." What could be more explicit? And who was there in England to question his facts?

And yet just before his last illness in 1866 Dr. Neale brought out a third edition of his *Hymns of the Eastern Church* with a new preface in which he said that " Art thou weary " and two of the other hymns " contain so little from the Greek, that they ought not to have been included in this collection; in any future Edition they shall appear as an Appendix."

We can imagine what had happened. He had been anxious to make out the best case he could for the Greek hymns as a link between the Greek and English Churches. But even to make them presentable he had to change and omit and piece together, and to water some doctrines too strong for English palates. In some of his translations a searcher would find it hard to identify his originals, and on reflection his conscience compelled him to confess that " Art thou weary " had no original at all. Possibly some phrase or mannerism of St. Stephen moved him to write it, but it was all his own.

Dr. Neale had made what the French call a *faux pas;* an unfortunate one because when a mistake once gets into circulation it is hard to correct. He did not live to remove the three hymns from his translations, and after his death his publishers did not help much. At least one edition of *Hymns of the Eastern Church* was printed just as he left it, and a fifth edition that did remove the hymn to an appendix printed there with it all the data about St. Stephen's authorship and even omitted Dr. Neale's little confession from the preface.

This explains no doubt why Mr. King, dealing with this hymn in his *Anglican Hymnology* of 1885, gives not only a biography of the Syrian monk but an account of a visit to the monastery of Mar Saba as " more endeared " to him when he remembers that " there eleven centuries ago St. Stephen wrote the touching hymn." All of which in his turn Mr. Duffield has copied into his *English Hymns* and Mr. Morrison in his turn into his *Great Hymns of the Church*. And so it happens that our little voyager still finds a harbor in many a Christian heart, flying the Greek flag under which it was launched in 1862.

SOME POINTS FOR DISCUSSION

1. The Church is a society of human beings, and almost as open to fluctuations of feeling and changes of opinion and manners as worldly society is. The Word of God does not change, but our response to it is always changing. The Church's hymn book is a sort of registering thermometer that first feels and then records these changes. And the hymn books of to-day show a very different face from those, say, of 1840. These changes are of course largely due to the Oxford Movement and the new ideals of churchliness it spread abroad, but in bringing them about Dr. Neale has had more influence than any other man. He linked the Church's hymns with the Church's history; for which achievement he alone of the men of his time had the requisite scholarship. He invested our congregational praise with something like an atmosphere of romance — the light of other days and glimpses of far-off things: he awakened the Church to a sense of " her unending song." And his matchless translations have actually made some hymns of the Middle Ages as familiar as household words.

When we remember how extreme and uncompromising Dr. Neale's High Church views were, it is amazing to find that in some denominations which once sang no hymns but those of Dr. Watts and still adhere in the main to Watts's theology, there are nearly as many of Dr. Neale's hymns in actual use to-day as of Watts himself. And the fact may properly raise the question whether he was not only the greatest personal influence in modifying our hymnody but also the greatest of the nineteenth century hymn writers.

2. The Evangelical hymn writer, Miss Havergal, says

in one of her letters that she " cannot understand how any Christian can stand still and sing such a misrepresentation of Christ's service as " are the words of the fourth verse, —

> If I find Him, if I follow,
> What His guerdon here?
> " Many a sorrow, many a labor,
> Many a tear."

" Is not that too bad? Do we not know it to be unfair to our Lord and His happy service? Where does He say that is ' His guerdon here '? Let us just think for our service what He does say: ' Work; for I am with you, saith the Lord of Hosts.' That alone is the grandest, richest, sweetest ' guerdon here ' that any loving heart can ask."

Is there any actual difference between the " work " which is a part of the guerdon here, according to Miss Havergal, and the " many a labor," which is a part of it, according to Dr. Neale? Is the saying " In this world ye shall have tribulation " to be separated from the " Work; for I am with you," or is Dr. Neale right in joining " many a labor " with " many a tear "? It may be that if Miss Havergal had been less impulsive and willing to " stand still " long enough to sing the hymn through, she might have come to feel that in verse four Dr. Neale was only laying the ground adroitly for the " sorrow vanquished " of verse five.

3. Of the tunes to this hymn in *The Hymnal revised* " Stephanos," the lower one, is that which first attracted attention to the words in *Hymns ancient and modern.* The melody was composed by the Rev. Sir Henry Williams Baker, editor-in-chief of that book, author also of

" The King of love my Shepherd is," and he asked Dr. Monk, the musical editor, to manage the harmonies for him. It is a good tune when sung deliberately and with feeling. Rattled off without feeling, by American voices especially, it becomes unpleasant and even acquires a nasal twang. Perhaps the fact that it is so often rattled off explains why many people have come to prefer the more sentimental tune of Dr. Bullinger.

To which tune was it that George Olver and Lute Cradlebow sang these words together? Having read *Cape Cod Folks*, the writer is confident they sang the tune provided in the Moody and Sankey *Gospel Hymns No. 2*. But does not Captain Satchell's description of their singing afford in itself clues enough to identify the tune?

XXI

SAVIOUR, AGAIN TO THY DEAR NAME WE RAISE

THE TEXT OF THE HYMN

1 Saviour, again to Thy dear Name we raise
   With one accord our parting hymn of praise;
   We stand to bless Thee ere our worship cease;
   Then, lowly kneeling, wait Thy word of peace.

2 Grant us Thy peace upon our homeward way;
   With Thee began, with Thee shall end the day:
   Guard Thou the lips from sin, the hearts from shame,
   That in this house have called upon Thy Name.

3 Grant us Thy peace, Lord, through the coming night;
   Turn Thou for us its darkness into light;
   From harm and danger keep Thy children free,
   For dark and light are both alike to Thee.

4 Grant us Thy peace throughout our earthly life,
   Our balm in sorrow, and our stay in strife;
   Then, when Thy voice shall bid our conflict cease,
   Call us, O Lord, to Thine eternal peace.

Rev. John Ellerton, 1866

NOTE: The text here given is that which was prepared for the
Appendix to *Hymns ancient and modern,* 1868. Other forms of the
hymn are referred to under " Some Points for Discussion."

A CHURCHLY HYMN

This is the third in our little group of High Church hymns, and anyone familiar with the history of the English Church and English hymns would know at a glance that it was inspired by the Oxford Movement. It is " churchly."

There is nothing romantic or striking in the origin of the hymn or in the life of the clergyman who wrote it. The interest lies rather in discovering the hymn to be so natural an expression of the author's personality and his relation to the Movement that we feel the writing of it to have been almost inevitable.

Some strange tales, hard to credit nowadays, are told of the neglected and sometimes disreputable conditions of public worship in English parish churches in the years before the Oxford Movement of the eighteen-thirties: tales of ancient buildings falling into decay and dirty, of furnishings shabby and unseemly, of sacraments administered carelessly and uncouthly, of scanty and irreverent congregations. With every allowance for exaggeration it is plain that the ordinance of worship was suffering from indifference.

To change all that was one of the very first tasks the High Church Party set for itself: to make the worship express visibly in dignity and even stateliness the high doctrines it held of Church and Sacrament. The extreme men aimed at more than this, at nothing less than to restore the full Catholic ceremonial: but in an insistence upon outward beauty and reverence and in giving more of a mystical tone to the celebration of Holy Communion, all High Churchmen were agreed. The brightening and embellishment of public worship became the visible sign and token of the Movement, as year by year it widened its bounds and gradually, against great opposition, changed the outward face of the Church of England.

This enrichment of the church services was the feature of the Movement that especially attracted the Rev. John Ellerton, author of " Saviour, again to Thy dear Name we raise." The hymn itself shows this. It could have been written only by one to whom the reverent conduct of public worship meant a great deal. Its very atmosphere is churchly. The " we " of the opening line makes us feel ourselves members of a church engaged in an act of corporate worship, now closing with a parting hymn of praise. Our very attitudes of body are portrayed. We stand to sing: we kneel for the benediction, and go out in the hush that follows God's word of peace. And the thought of the hymn is that lips and heart so engaged in reverent offices should carry with them to the life outside the peace of that benediction and the purity of that worship.

THE AUTHOR OF THE HYMN

John Ellerton was born in a refined and religious home in London nine days before the Christmas of 1826. There had come to the city, shortly before a young Presbyterian minister from Scotland, Edward Irving. Tall, white-faced, long-haired, an orator and enthusiast, his preaching took the religious world by storm; a great Presbyterian church was built for him at Regent Square, and he became the fashionable preacher of London. Feeling himself a prophet to Babylon the Great, his message soon took the shape of heralding the imminent return of the Messiah, and was accompanied by a revival of the miraculous gifts of the Apostolic Church. As his eloquence grew less coherent, and " the tongues " began to make themselves heard in unearthly shrieks and unintelligible " prophecies," he lost his vogue, was deposed by the Church of Scotland, and faded out of notice by the general public.

The excited interest Irving had aroused in millenarian speculations, and the expectation of the Second Advent, still continued among the London Evangelicals. Mr. Ellerton tells us that in the religious circle in which his boyhood was spent, the favorite and inexhaustible subject of talk and reading was unfulfilled prophecy. The chronology of the future was a chief concern: in what year would the Jews be restored, Papacy be destroyed, the Millenium begin? The shy and sensitive boy drank it all in and awaited with perfect faith some great crisis predicted for 1844. He was shocked when in 1841 his father executed a seven-year lease of some real estate. These religious speculations he soon left behind, but a deep love for the Evangelical type of piety he had witnessed at home stayed with him all his life, and served as a corrective of later High Church opinions.

At eighteen he was sent up to Cambridge University, into a changed atmosphere, where the center of debate was not the marks of the Beast but the marks of the true church. Here he came under the influence of Frederick Denison Maurice, a Broad rather than High Church theologian. And so it happened that as Mr. Ellerton fell in gradually with the views of the new High Church Party, his Evangelical heritage and the liberal doctrines of Maurice diluted them. He was never tempted to go to such extremes as Dr. Neale.

In these matters of opinion Mr. Ellerton, like most of us, was a mirror rather than a shining light, reflecting more or less of surrounding influences. So far as his

THE REV. JOHN ELLERTON

outward career is concerned he was simply a typical English country parson, important in his parish, not widely influential outside: but something more than we mean when in this country we speak of a country minister.

In England the Church is a part of the political system. The whole surface is plotted into a network of parishes, each with a parish church and a parish clergyman, supported by taxes levied on the products of soil and industry. At its best the system secures to each parish the residence of a refined and educated gentleman as a friend of the poor and a sort of spiritual squire; the parson has a social status and his lot often falls in very pleasant places. There are hard places, too; parishes remote, rude, or too poor to furnish even a decent living, or where the only people who might make a congregation in the parish church prefer to go to dissenting chapels, or the man who owns perhaps the whole parish is hostile to the church or parson.

Mr. Ellerton's lot lay largely in obscure but apparently not hard places. He began in 1850 with three years in a Sussex village, followed by an assistant ministry in one of the Brighton churches. From there he passed on to one country parish and another, four in all. He was stricken with paralysis at the end of 1891, retired to Torquay and died there on June 15, 1893. When lying disabled he was nominated to a prebendary's stall of St. Alban's Cathedral, the only recognition that ever came to him; an honor empty enough, but entitling him under some peculiar custom of that cathedral to be addressed during the last months of his illness as " Canon " Ellerton.

THE STORY OF THE HYMN

Always and everywhere Mr. Ellerton was first of all the faithful parson, but he had also ample opportunity to cultivate a hobby. And his hobby was hymns. From being a hobby they grew into a controlling interest of

Evening
[*After Service, Sundays or Festivals*]

Saviour; again to Thy dear name we raise
With one accord our parting hymn of praise.
We stand to bless Thee ere our worship cease.
Then, lowly kneeling, wait Thy word of peace.

Grant us Thy peace through this approaching night;
Turn Thou for us its darkness into light;
From harm and danger keep Thy children free,
For dark and light are both alike to Thee.

Grant us Thy peace upon our homeward way;
With Thee began, with Thee shall end the day:
Guard Thou the lips from sin, the hearts from shame
That in this house have called upon Thy name.

Grant us Thy peace throughout our earthly life,
Our balm in sorrow, and our stay in strife;
Then, when Thy voice shall bid our conflict cease,
Call us, O Lord, to Thine eternal peace.
                                        Amen.

Nantwich Church
1866

AUTOGRAPH OF THE HYMN

his life — the study of hymns, the preparation of hymn books, and most of all hymn writing. He had begun writing them for his Sunday school while assistant at Brighton, just as Dr. Bonar had done while assistant at Leith; and, like Dr. Bonar again, he published a chil-

dren's hymn book. He went on writing hymns throughout his life, and five years before his death gathered them
into a volume of *Hymns original and translated*. They
were not sudden inspirations or flashes of poetic fire.
They were planned and wrought as contributions to the
new hymnody of his Church; sometimes to fit an occasion, sometimes to supply a gap in the provision for special days of the Prayer Book.

"Saviour, again to Thy dear Name we raise" was
written at Crewe Green in 1866, to be sung at a festival
of parish choirs held in Nantwich. Like others of his
hymns it was composed to fit a particular tune that
took his fancy and ran in his head; in this case a tune
called "St. Agnes" he found in a recently published collection of Edward H. Thorne. Mr. F. A. Jones, who
made a diligent search for the original manuscripts of
familiar hymns, tells us it was written on the reverse of
a leaf of the sermon preached the Sunday before, and
that in the first draft the opening line read:

"Father, once more before we part, we raise."

As Mr. Ellerton wrote it, there were six verses; at one
time or another it has been revised, by his own hand
and the hands of other people also, so that several differing texts are current. When that 1868 Appendix to
Hymns ancient and modern was planned (the one that
took in some of Dr. Neale's hymns of the Greek Church),
Mr. Ellerton sent in this hymn to the editors, and either
he or they prepared the abridgment in four verses as
there printed, which is still the most familiar text. A
little later he became one of the editors of the rival
Church Hymns of 1871 and prepared for it a different
form of the hymn, a facsimile of which is here given.

One wonders why he wished the " approaching night " verse to have precedence over the " homeward way " verse, and why he preferred the harsh " through this approaching night " to " through the coming night." But even hymn writers have their little obstinacies.

With the hymn thus lodged in both the important hymnals, its future in the Church of England was secure. When it was taken from *Hymns ancient and modern* into the *Presbyterian Hymnal* published at Philadelphia in 1874, many good Presbyterians, who knew very little about the Oxford Movement and had supposed that Watts, the Wesleys and the Evangelicals wrote all the good hymns, must have wondered sometimes from what source the editor of their new book drew such hymns as this and " Jerusalem the golden " and " The Church's one Foundation."

SOME POINTS FOR DISCUSSION

1. Mr. Ellerton was among the most accomplished of the men who wrote churchly hymns in the latter half of the nineteenth century. The whole number of his is just short of a hundred, and many of them are in actual use. All are marked by deep reverence and by feeling carefully restrained within the limits of what may be expected from average worshipers. They vary much in quality, and some of those for saints' days and special occasions carry marks of manufacture. Whence indeed could one draw inspiration for the commemoration of St. Bartholomew, of whom we do not know a thing, or for " Catechising " or for " The Sunday after a funeral " ?

Of the thirteen of Ellerton's hymns (aside from the two in which he had some part) in *The Hymnal revised* which are the best? And are there any that could be spared?

2. Anyone interested in the text of the hymn should examine the form given in *The New Hymnal* of the Protestant Episcopal Church (1916). It is in four verses made up from the six as originally written, and the third verse much extends the scope of the peace prayed for, as follows:

> Grant us Thy peace throughout our earthly life;
> Peace to Thy Church from error and from strife;
> Peace to our land, the fruit of truth and love;
> Peace in each heart, Thy Spirit from above.

3. Of the tunes for this hymn in *The Hymnal revised,* "Pax Dei" is the original setting composed by Dr. Dykes for the Appendix of 1868; and Mr. F. A. Jones quotes Mrs. Ellerton as saying that her husband was so delighted with it that he sent the composer a letter of thanks. It has been retained in all later issues of *Hymns ancient and modern,* amounting now to many millions of copies, and is sung the wide world over.

Dr. Hopkins' "Ellers," originally named "Benediction," and written in 1869 for unison singing with varied harmonies, was chosen for *Church Hymns,* and is certainly an ideal tune for congregational use. Mr. Ellerton told his biographer that he had come to prefer it (when sung in unison) to Dr. Dykes's tune. Having both before us we are as free as Mr. Ellerton was to make our personal choice — and to change it.

XXII

THE CHURCH'S ONE FOUNDATION

THE TEXT OF THE HYMN

1 The Church's one Foundation
   Is Jesus Christ her Lord;
   She is His new creation
   By water and the word:
   From heaven He came and sought her
   To be His holy Bride;
   With His own blood He bought her,
   And for her life He died.

2 Elect from every nation,
   Yet one o'er all the earth,
   Her charter of salvation
   One Lord, one faith, one birth;
   One holy Name she blesses,
   Partakes one holy food,
   And to one hope she presses,
   With every grace endued.

3 Though with a scornful wonder
   Men see her sore oppressed,
   By schisms rent asunder,
   By heresies distressed,
   Yet saints their watch are keeping,
   Their cry goes up, "How long?"
   And soon the night of weeping
   Shall be the morn of song.

4 'Mid toil and tribulation,
   And tumult of her war,
   She waits the consummation
   Of peace for evermore;

Till with the vision glorious
    Her longing eyes are blest,
And the great Church victorious
    Shall be the Church at rest.

5 Yet she on earth hath union
    With God the Three in One,
And mystic sweet communion
    With those whose rest is won:
O happy ones and holy!
    Lord, give us grace that we,
Like them the meek and lowly,
    On high may dwell with Thee.

Rev. Samuel John Stone, 1866

NOTE: As originally printed in the author's *Lyra Fidelium* the hymn had seven verses. Of these the third (hereinafter quoted) is here omitted as polemical, and the sixth and seventh are combined, greatly to their advantage, in one verse. There is, however, no change in the text itself.

Does it not seem quaint that a pronounced High Churchman, wishing to teach his people what the Church really is, should write for them a hymn embodying practically every doctrine concerning the Church he held most dear (its divine origin, its unbroken continuity, its catholicity and essential unity, its orthodoxy, its sacramental grace, its communion with God and with the departed saints, its militancy and final triumph), and then that his hymn should be welcomed not only by his own party but by his Low Church opponents, and by almost all communions or denominations or sects that believe in the Church at all, quite without regard to the particular opinions they hold and promulgate as to church history and doctrine, church authority, or church organization?

It is indeed a very extraordinary happening; and the writer has sometimes asked himself by what magic it came about. Was the author "Catholic" in a larger sense than he was aware of? It is possible. Or are all the denominations of Christians becoming High Church? No: that could not be claimed, though all or most have felt the effects of the Oxford Movement. The writer has concluded that the explanation of the hymn's general acceptance lies in the fact that all its statements of doctrine are made in the words and phrases of Scripture itself, and thus every denomination is left free to interpret the statements of the hymn in the same terms in which it interprets the texts on which those statements are based.

THE STORY OF THE HYMN

This hymn was written by the Rev. Samuel John Stone, then beginning his ministry as assistant or curate in the town of Windsor. Windsor in on the Thames, twenty-one miles from London, with the royal castle looking down upon it, and across the river, a bit to the north, Eton College, the most famous boys' school in England. Mr. Stone's work was largely among the poorer people in the outskirts, where he had a mission chapel of his own.

He has said that the hymn really grew out of the state of feeling aroused by the "Colenso Controversy." Bishop Colenso, of South Africa, had published a book denying the historical accuracy of the first five books of the Bible, known as the Pentateuch. His metropolitan bishop, Dr. Gray, deposed him from office, and when an appeal to England was taken, Mr. Stone shared the intense excitement of the controversy that followed. He felt that Colenso was undermining "the Catholic faith," approved of Bishop Gray's course, and deplored the schism Colenso's followers made in the South African Church.

That accounts for a heated verse in the hymn as first printed, now happily dropped out:

> "The Church shall never perish!
> Her dear Lord to defend,
> To guide, sustain, and cherish
> Is with her to the end:
> Though there be those who hate her,
> And false sons in her pale,
> Against or foe or traitor
> She ever shall prevail: "

and also for the lines still retained:

> "Though with a scornful wonder
> Men see her sore oppressed,
> By schisms rent asunder,
> By heresies distrest: "

So much for the hymn's origin; and now for the use which its author found for it. He noticed that the cottagers at Windsor were given to saying the Apostles' Creed as one of their private prayers, though without clear ideas of what its various articles meant. This suggested the writing of a series of hymns that would explain them, and could be used at home or in the chapel. And he printed in 1866 *Lyra Fidelium. Twelve Hymns on the twelve articles of the Apostles' Creed. By S. J. Stone, B. A., Curate of Windsor.* "The Church's one Foundation" is headed:

ARTICLE IX.

"The Holy Catholic Church: the Communion of Saints."
"He is the Head of the Body, the Church."

and on the opposite page is a prose "Summary of Truths confessed in Article IX," followed by what the Westminster Catechism would call "the Scripture proofs."

AUTOGRAPH LINES OF THE HYMN

How far Mr. Stone's cottagers were edified we do not know, but the hymn was taken into that same 1868 Appendix to *Hymns ancient and modern* of which we have already heard, and there set to the tune "Aurelia" to which it has been sung ever since. The statement that "Aurelia" was composed for these words is mistaken. It was written earlier as a setting for "Jerusalem the golden." The conjunction of hymn and tune was one of many happy things done by the editors of the Appendix, and so joined they at once proceeded on their triumphant way to become the marching song of the Church. The only danger that threatens the continuance of that career is the fatigue that waits on too constant repetition. An English archbishop said that wherever called to open or dedicate a church, he could always count on two things — cold chicken and " The Church's one Foundation." To which the obvious retort is, " There is nothing better."

"A VERAY PARFIT GENTIL KNIGHT"

We could wish for a portrait of the young curate who wrote the hymn. Perhaps the one we have of his full maturity is not less interesting. It is the photograph of a sturdy, full-blooded, broad-shouldered and athletic English gentleman (English all over). His clothes reveal the clergyman: we might have thought him an admiral. A physiognomist could " deduce " a good deal more from the leonine moulding of the head, the strong straight nose, the piercing but kindly eye and general air of command: more yet if the photographer had not obliterated the lines of character and experience, and the little crinkles of humor also that were surely there.

It is no surprise to learn that he had a quick temper, and that like his " gentle " Master, who laid the whip on the money changers, he was capable of a righteous wrath that was serious. There was an occasion in a lonely East End locality when he came upon three blackguards attacking a poor unfriended girl. Stone heard her cries, rushed to her help, knocked out the first man with one blow, turned to the second and trounced him until he cried for mercy, and ever after regretted that the third got off before he could catch him. He told a companion he thanked God he had learned to use his fists at Charterhouse and would have given five pounds to get at the third rascal's hide. Then, seeing a quizzical look in his companion's eye and recalling clerical

THE REV. SAMUEL JOHN STONE

proprieties, he burst into hearty laughter directed wholly against himself. We all love Don Quixote.

And Mr. Stone was nearer the ideal of a knight, with his innate purity of soul, his chivalry, his hatred of wrong, his unselfishness, and his spotless life, than he was to the type of the " muscular Christian." He had a sensitive temperament, " the muscles of a prize-fighter and the nerves of a violin," his doctor said: he was emotional and excitable, with an active brain and a very tender heart. It was his way to idealize his friends, his country, his church, and all womankind; but especially his Queen, the type to him of motherhood and sovereignty in one, whom he loved and extolled, and if need be defended, with a boyish devotion and heat.

The boy that continued to live in him till pretty near the end was born at Whitmore, Staffordshire, in April, 1839, and had the good fortune for the first thirteen years of his life to be a country boy; his father being parson of one and another rural parish. Then his family moved to London, and he was sent to the same Charterhouse that Thackeray loved and made famous. From there he went to Pembroke College, Oxford, and distinguished himself in athletics at least, becoming captain of his college boat, entered heartily into the Volunteer Movement just beginning, and made a try for the poetry prize. The boy's whole bent was toward soldiering, and it was only the " one clear call for me " that turned the man's face toward the ministry.

His began in 1862 with a curacy at Windsor of nearly eight years. Then he went back to London to help his father in an East End parish, St. Paul's, Haggerston. It was a thickly populated parish without a well-to-do person within its bounds, its worst street on the lowest stratum of London poverty. And in it Mr. Stone, first as his father's assistant and then as his successor, spent twenty years of pastoral life, unselfishly laboring from early morning till late at night to meet the spiritual needs of his parishioners, to educate their children in the parish schools, and to get a bit of brightness into hard lives. His combination of virility and sympathy gave him real power over the people. He was a churchman rather than a missionary, a shepherd rather than an evangelist; and St. Paul's, Haggerston, was the door of the fold. But there was none of the ritualism there with which many earnest workers appeal to the East End.

In a bit of garden back of the parsonage is a dog's grave, and this epitaph:

> In the centre of this lawn lies
> SANCHO
> a gentleman in all but humanity; thoroughbred,
> single in mind, true of heart; for seventeen years
> the faithful and affectionate friend of his master,
> who loved him, and now for him "faintly trusts
> the larger Hope," contained, it may be, in Romans
> viii. 19–21.
> He died April 26, 1883.

It is a memorial of Mr. Stone as well as of Sancho. And it reminds us of a similar but much statelier monument to a dog in the garden of one of our Walnut Street mansions in Philadelphia, whose doors have never opened since the dog's master passed through them, now many years ago.

By 1890 Mr. Stone had worn himself out. An easier post was found for him in one of the surviving churches of old London "City," All Hallows, London Wall; a quaint, musty little church packed away amid great blocks of offices and warehouses, which he first made beautiful and then proceeded to make useful, in a parish swarming with workers all day and at night populated only by care-takers and their families. One use he made of the building was criticized, but was much appreciated by a great number of girls who for economy's sake came up to Liverpool Street by the early workmen's trains and had to wander about the streets till their places of work were opened. He threw the church open from 6:30 to 8:30 each morning as a haven in which they could sit and wait. Reading of books (not newspapers) and sewing were allowed but no talking or eating. And to many of the girls the house of rest became a house of prayer.

For the last of his ten years at All Hallows Mr. Stone endured the increasing agonies of cancer, and he died on November 19, 1900. On the 23rd many of the thronging business men who hurried by the little church must have caught the strains of his funeral hymn, "The Church's one Foundation."

Among his devoted friends Mr. Stone had one, an accomplished man of letters, Mr. Coulson Kernahan. Resolving to attempt some memorial of a man whom he esteemed so great, Mr. Kernahan waited sixteen years, for fear that his affection would tempt him to exaggerate, and then printed a graphic characterization of Mr. Stone, which the present writer wishes could be read by all young people who feel no impulse to follow in the train of anæmic saints but can recognize a hero even under a tall hat.

Mr. Kernahan, with a true artist's instinct, discloses frankly those frailties or limitations that reveal his friend as human, and, as an essential part of him, become almost lovable: the fixedness of his ideas; the perfect confidence in his own beliefs and opinions that made him seem obstinate; the irascibility of overstrained nerves; an impatience of opposition that made him sometimes overbearing; a certain hot-headedness that interfered with cool judgment; his unbending Toryism and stiff churchmanship and incapacity of understanding how an English gentleman could feel otherwise; and a constitutional inability to see anything wrong in those he loved and trusted that occasionally got him into trouble.

And then, over these little shadows (how slight they are made to seem) Mr. Kernahan throws the light of his friend's moral splendor in a tribute as heartfelt and as noble as was ever given to mortal man:

" So brave of heart was he as to make possible for us the courage of a Coeur de Lion, so knightly of nature as to make possible the honor of an Arthur or a Galahad, so nearly stainless in the standard he set himself, in the standard he attained, as to come, as near as human flesh and blood can come, almost to making possible the purity of the Christ."

SOME POINTS FOR DISCUSSION

1. There is a small group of familiar hymns that do not take the form of praise or prayer or exhortation, but the form of teaching. They are called didactic hymns, and consist of a series of statements setting forth some doctrine. This, setting forth the doctrine of the Church, Bishop Wordsworth's " Gracious Spirit, Holy Ghost," expounding the doctrine of Love, and his " O day of rest and gladness," setting forth the history and benefits of the Christian Sunday, are examples.

The number of successful didactic hymns is small. It takes a cunning hand and a warm glow to overcome our instinct against going to school when we are asked to sing praise. Of Mr. Stone's twelve hymns on the Creed, only this and " Weary of earth and laden with my sin " have come into use, and the latter is hardly didactic. But " The Church's one Foundation " uses this form and manner triumphantly. What other didactic hymns are familiar?

2. When Mr. Stone printed *Lyra Fidelium* for his cottagers, against each line or couplet of the hymns he set on the opposite page the texts on which it was based. Here are the four texts set opposite the four couplets of the first verse of our hymn.

" Other foundation can no man lay than is laid, which is Jesus Christ."

" Except a man be born of water and of the Spirit, he cannot enter into the kingdom of God."

" Even as Christ also loved the Church and gave Himself for it, that He might sanctify and cleanse it."

" The Church of God which He purchased with His own Blood."

Some readers might find an interest in supplying equally suitable " proof texts " for the other verses.

3. The weaving of Scriptural truth and church doctrine into strains of song was Mr. Stone's special gift in hymn writing. His hymns, as gathered shortly before his death, number fifty-five, many of which are in use in his own communion, not many outside of it. He published also three volumes of poetry, creditable to his head and heart; but the writer would not care to have Mr. Kernahan ask him how many of the leaves in his copies

have been cut open. He does not find Mr. Stone's poetry at all convincing, and he thinks it would be a mistake to regard "The Church's one Foundation" as a poem. It is good verse and full of feeling, but of spiritual and not poetic feeling. So the writer thinks, but the question is open for discussion: remembering, however, that while rhythm makes verse only imagination makes poetry.

XXIII

O LOVE THAT WILT NOT LET ME GO

THE TEXT OF THE HYMN

1.   O Love that wilt not let me go,
    I rest my weary soul in Thee;
    I give Thee back the life I owe,
    That in Thine ocean depths its flow
      May richer, fuller be.

2.   O Light that followest all my way,
    I yield my flickering torch to Thee;
    My heart restores its borrowed ray,
    That in Thy sunshine's blaze its day
      May brighter, fairer be.

3.   O Joy that seekest me through pain
    I cannot close my heart to Thee;
    I trace the rainbow through the rain,
    And feel the promise is not vain
      That morn shall tearless be.

4.   O Cross that liftest up my head,
    I dare not ask to fly from Thee;
    I lay in dust life's glory dead,
    And from the ground there blossoms red
      Life that shall endless be.

Rev. George Matheson, 1882

NOTE: The text is taken from *The Scottish Hymnal* of 1885, with the change in one line made for that book by the author.

One of the effects of the High Church Movement in Episcopalian England, whose hymns we have been studying, was to make a considerable number of the clergy of Presbyterian Scotland very much dissatisfied with the architecture and worship of their parish churches and the meager allowance of hymns which supplemented the metrical Psalms. They formed a Church Service Society which brought about many changes, and they put through *The Scottish Hymnal,* with Dr. Monk, who had done such great things in *Hymns ancient and modern,* in charge of its musical side. This book changed the face of hymnody in the Church of Scotland to the Anglican model. The enlarged edition of the book in 1885 gave to the Church for the first time the hymn we are now studying with its " proper tune "; the words having appeared in a church periodical a year or so before. So there is just that much connection (and no more) between the High Church Movement and the present hymn.

THE STORY OF THE HYMN

The hymn was written by the Rev. George Matheson, minister of the parish of Innellan in the Church of Scotland.

Dr. Matheson was a large and many-sided personality, of a powerful mind touched with genius, of great attainments and with a distinguished career. It may therefore seem far fetched to present him here as the author of a single hymn, which in fact was thrown off in a few minutes, as though the hymn was the center of his career and his most characteristic performance. And yet such is the simple truth.

Very much the same thing happened in the case of the great poet, Tennyson, to whom " Sunset and Evening Star " came without volition and was also thrown off in a few minutes. The poet at once recognized it as the crown of his art and the measure of his faith, and directed that it be printed at the close of every edition of his works, as their culmination.

Dr. Matheson's whole personality and deepest experiences are behind the hymn: it is the most perfect expression of the man at his highest: and it is the high-water mark in his career as a writer. He was constantly printing religious verses, and yet he knew quite well that this hymn was a thing apart. Its writing, he said, was " to me a unique experience. I have no natural gift of rhythm. All the other verses I have ever written are manufactured articles; this came like a dayspring from on high. I have never been able to gain once more the same fervor in verse."

We have his own account of the circumstances:

"My hymn was composed in the manse of Innellan, on the evening of 6th June, 1882. I was at that time alone. It was the day of my sister's marriage, and the rest of the family were staying over night in Glasgow. Something had happened to me, which was known only to myself, and which caused me the most severe mental suffering. The hymn was the fruit of that suffering. It was the quickest bit of work I ever did in my life. I had the impression rather of having it dictated to me by some inward voice than of working it out myself. I am quite sure that the whole work was completed in five minutes, and equally sure that it never received at my hands any retouching or correction. The Hymnal Committee of the Church of Scotland desired the change of

one word. I had written originally ' I climbed the rainbow in the rain.' They objected to the word ' climb '
and I put in ' trace.' "

The nature of the personal sorrow behind the hymn
Dr. Matheson did not disclose, and we may respect his
reticence. The statement one has read that it was the
failure of the love of the woman to whom he was engaged
on learning the doctor's verdict of impending blindness,
her curt refusal " to go through life with a blind man,"
may be ignored, as he had been " a blind man " for
twenty-five years.

The success of the hymn was largely due to the
tune " St. Margaret," written for it by Dr. Albert L.
Peace, then organist of Glasgow Cathedral and musical
editor of *The Scottish Hymnal* of 1885. He did for
Matheson's words what Dr. Dykes's " Lux Benigna "
did for Cardinal Newman's " Lead, kindly Light." It
was his habit to carry about with him the words of the
hymns for which tunes were needed. Sitting on the
sands of Arran and reading these, he tells us, the tune
came upon him like a flash, and, taking out his pencil,
he wrote it off in a few minutes.

For a while the use of the hymn was confined to the
Church of Scotland and its preaching stations on the continent of Europe and elsewhere. From more than one
of these word came to the present writer, while preparing *The Hymnal* of 1895, of the deep impression hymn
and music had made upon one or another American
tourist, with an earnest request that they might not fail
of a place in the new book. Such a letter from as far
as Cairo, dated in April of 1895, lies under the writer's
eye as he pens these words.

THE AUTHOR OF THE HYMN

George Matheson was born in Glasgow, March 27, 1842; the son of a prosperous merchant there. His was not therefore the heritage of poverty out of which so many eminent Scottish clergymen have won their way. There are, however, far worse handicaps than poverty, and one of them is blindness. Even as a child his sight was impaired by inflammation back of his eyes. At school he could still read by the aid of powerful glasses, but from his entrance to the University of Glasgow in 1857, his sight failed him altogether, and we have to think of a buoyant and eager boy, the best student in his school, with all a scholar's instincts and ambitions, facing a life fettered if not thwarted. He entered at once the spiritual struggle his situation made inevitable, he put to Heaven the old and unanswered question of why a catastrophe so undeserved should befall him. Happily he stood the test of his faith and won the Christian secret of submission and something already of the self-surrender of which his beautiful hymn was to sing.

Matheson's blindness has been regarded by some as an endowment, a blessing in disguise, that made possible all that he became and the real spiritual influence he exerted. Others regard it as seriously affecting his full development, and as the obstacle that prevented his becoming the great Scottish churchman of his time, and the spiritual leader of his generation. Who can say? What we know is that he had a brave and useful life, became a successful preacher of a very high order, and by his devotional and other books influenced for good a great number of people. Looking back upon his career, he himself called it "an obstructed life, a circumscribed life, but a life of boundless sanguineness, a life of quenchless hopefulness, a life which has beaten persistently against the cage of circumstance, and which even at the time of abandoned work has said not 'Good night,' but 'Good morning.'"

Quite possibly, if he had had his sight, he would have followed his inclination to study law. He would have proved a great advocate surely, a great lawyer it may be, though not so assuredly. As things were he entered the ministry of the Church of Scotland, to which his family had adhered at the Disruption, and was licensed by the Presbytery of Glasgow in June, 1866.

His first parish was Innellan, then a small place and something of a summer retreat, on the Firth of Clyde. There was strong opposition to a blind minister; but he soon won all hearts, proved a capable pastor, and remained there for eighteen years, with ever-spreading reputation as a preacher of very unusual power, even for Scotland, the land of great preachers.

Dr. Matheson first came before the general public as a scientific theologian, with his *Aids to the study of German Theology* in 1874, and three years later with his *The Growth of the Spirit of Christianity*, a brilliant book with marked defects. Some of its mistakes were pointed out by critics, and its author was charged with being an inaccurate student. One of his friends has referred to the effect these criticisms had upon the author himself. "When he saw that for the purposes of scholarship his blindness was a fatal hindrance, he withdrew from the field — not without pangs, but finally." ("Abandoned work" already; and now to "say Good morning.")

He next undertook blithely the task of a reconciler
between the old faith and the new learning — evolution
and the higher criticism of the Bible. But gradually
his own mind became tangled in the perplexities and con-
tradictions he sought to solve, and he could not see his
way. In the end he turned his back on these problems,
and apparently on the new learning itself, and retired
within his own soul to renew the fires of faith and deepen
the inner life of communion with God. ("Abandoned
work" again, and again "Good morning.") His later
books are expository and devotional; glowing, mystical
and deeply spiritual, as of a prophet seeing things in-
visible, and trying to narrate his vision.

Before leaving Innellan he had the honor, dear to the
hearts of the clergy of the established Church, of being
summoned to Balmoral to preach before Her Majesty,
Queen Victoria, a Presbyterian while residing in Scotland and a communicant in her parish church of Craigie.
She wrote afterwards that she was " *immensely* delighted
with the sermon and the prayers," and with her usual
thoughtfulness she substituted for the customary signed
photograph a little bust of herself that the preacher
could feel.

In the fulness of his powers Matheson accepted a call
to Edinburgh, and in March, 1886, was installed as minister of St. Bernard's Parish Church, with some 1500
communicants. Here he repeated his earlier success on
a larger scale, and became a shining light, seen of all
men, waited upon by great congregations, honored by
the Scottish universities and esteemed in all the churches.
We have a description of him in the pulpit of St. Bernard's, as observed by the Rev. Charles Parkhurst of
New York: ' He enters the pulpit not larger than a

THE REV. GEORGE MATHESON

flour barrel. He has the face and form of General Grant, when the hero of Vicksburg was most stout, but is taller. With natural open eye you would not have thought he was blind. Now he rises, swaying a little until he gets his equilibrium. Announcing a Psalm for alternate reading, he takes his verses without the mistake of a word, and throughout the whole service, calling for several hymns and Scripture references with chapter and verse, he never made an error. Then he prays, and such a prayer! It seems profane to write about it. Though his sight is eclipsed he does see God, he does see into the hearts of his people. For forty minutes he preached on the text, " Holy men of God spake as they were moved by the Holy Ghost." We were instructed, refreshed, inspired.'

Dr. Matheson continued at St. Bernard's for thirteen years, when the burden became too heavy. His last years were spent in preparing more books and in preaching at large. He died during a summer holiday at North Berwick on August 28, 1906. He had never married, and was buried in his family's vault at Glasgow.

SOME POINTS FOR DISCUSSION

1. The hymn, let it be remembered, is autobiographical: the consecration of a great soul rising above the despondency caused by a calamity. If sung at all by the average Christian it should be sung very prayerfully. To sing it flippantly would be an act of pure hypocrisy. Even so its full meaning cannot be grasped without study. It seems worth while, therefore, to print here an analysis made by the Rev. Sydney Smith of Keith shortly after Dr. Matheson's death: —

" The unceasing appeal which the love of God makes to the soul, the truth that God loved us into being, that as we owe our life to Him, so it is only in love of Him that we find rest, only in service of Him that our life attains fullness — these are the thoughts with which the singer starts on his flight:

> " O Love that wilt not let me go,
>   I rest my weary soul in Thee;
> I give Thee back the life I owe,
> That in Thine ocean depths its flow
>   May richer, fuller be.

" That whatever light we have is but a spark from the central fire, that the divine Light ever shines and never fades, that the unsteady little lights by which we grope may sometimes dim its dawning glory, that by quenching them so as to let the Eternal Light shine, it does shine more and more unto the perfect day, that in God's light we see light — are some of the ideas to which the poet next gives expression:

> " O Light that followest all my way,
>   I yield my flickering torch to Thee;
> My heart restores its borrowed ray,
> That in Thy sunshine's blaze its day
>   May brighter, fairer be.

" Then the poet, turning his eye inward, is conscious of a mysterious joy mingling with and transfiguring his grief, a joy which, however absorbed he is in sorrow, will force itself upon him again and again, he sees a shimmer of meaning and mercy in the darkness of his lot, he beholds a bow in the cloud, giving assurance that the destroying flood will cease.

> "O Joy that seekest me through pain,
> I cannot close my heart to Thee;
> I trace the rainbow through the rain,
> And feel the promise is not vain
> That morn shall tearless be.

" The poet is convinced that it is so. As in the Light that ' followeth all his way,' he sees his cross to be his crown, he must not impatiently ask deliverance from the burden, he entreats power to make in the spirit of trust the sacrifice to which God plainly calls him:

> "I lay in dust life's glory dead,
> And from the ground there blossoms red
> Life that shall endless be."

It was in allusion to these last lines that a group of clergymen, who had sometime served as Dr. Matheson's assistants, sent to his funeral a wreath of red roses.

2. When Dr. Matheson is made to state that he originally wrote " I climbed the rainbow in the rain," we have perhaps an illustration of how hard it is for a blind scholar to secure entire accuracy. He must have meant " climb," one would think. Shall we agree with the Scottish Hymnal Committee that " I trace the rainbow through the rain " is the better line?

3. While speaking of accuracy it may be as well to note that the fourth word of the hymn, so often printed " will," is " wilt," and that it could not be anything else. It is only a seasoned poet, such as Dr. Holmes was, who would venture to print,

> "O Love Divine, that *stooped* to share."

A poet whose reputation was still in the making would probably have heard and heeded the call to write " stoopedest." But what a mouthful it is!

XXIV

GOD BE WITH YOU TILL WE MEET AGAIN

THE TEXT OF THE HYMN

1 God be with you till we meet again,
   By His counsels guide, uphold you,
   With His sheep securely fold you,
 God be with you till we meet again.
   Till we meet, till we meet,
   Till we meet at Jesus' feet;
   Till we meet, till we meet
 God be with you till we meet again.

2 God be with you till we meet again,
   'Neath His wings protecting hide you,
   Daily manna still divide you,
 God be with you till we meet again.
   Till we meet, *etc.*

3 God be with you till we meet again,
   When life's perils thick confound you,
   Put His arms unfailing round you,
 God be with you till we meet again.
   Till we meet, *etc.*

4 God be with you till we meet again,
   Keep love's banner floating o'er you,
   Smite death's threatening wave before you,
 God be with you till we meet again.
   Till we meet, *etc.*

Rev. Jeremiah Eames Rankin, 1880

We have now completed the studies of what we may call nineteenth century church hymns, and they have shown a progressive movement to improve the literary quality of the hymnody and to make it more " churchly."

But the tale is not yet told. The Church included a goodly proportion of those plain people of whom " God made so many "; who are loyal, but without special addiction to culture or churchliness. And among them began the movement, with which we are all familiar, to supplement the church hymns with popular religious songs, of a lighter type of words and music. From the evangelistic hymn book of Mr. Moody's campaign, the new songs took the name of " Gospel Hymns," and in course of time some of them have become very " Familiar Hymns." With a representative of these our studies may fitly close: most fitly perhaps with " God be with you," because it is the most familiar and because it is also a song at parting.

THE STORY OF THE HYMN

The hymn was written by a Congregationalist clergyman, Dr. Jeremiah Eames Rankin, while a pastor in Washington, D. C. After it became popular he was often asked about its origin. If his correspondents expected to hear that it came forth from a fine frenzy of feeling or under romantic circumstances, they must have been disappointed with his reply. At all events we have the actual facts from the author's own pen.

This is from a letter to Mr. H. Porter Smith, about 1890:

" God be With You, like most of my hymns and poems, was the product of a cool purpose, and not the result of

God Be With You Till We Meet Again

1. God be with you, till we meet again,
   By His counsels guide, uphold you,
   With His sheep securely fold you;
   God be with you, till we meet again.

Chorus: Till we meet at Jesus feet,
   God be with you, till we meet again

2. God be with you till we meet again,
   'Neath His wings protecting hide you,
   Daily manna still divide you:
   God be with you till we meet again.

3. God be with you till we meet again,
   When life's perils thick confound you,
   Put His arms unfailing round you;
   God be with you, till we meet again.

4. God be with you, till we meet again,
   Keep love's banner floating o'er you,
   Smite death's threat'ning wave before you;
   God be with you, till we meet again.

J.E. Rankin

AUTOGRAPH OF THE HYMN

any experience or feeling. The thought that that was the meaning of our honest and hearty greeting, 'Good by' was the germ of it. I tried to put into a hymn that thing, making it Christian instead of common. I was at the time getting up a gospel hymn book for use in my church in Washington, at the night service.

"Having written one stanza, I sent it to the author of What a Friend We Have in Jesus, and also to another man, some of whose melodies had pleased me. This last gentleman, Mr. Tomer, sent me back the present music of the hymn. It was put into shape a little — arranged, perhaps musicians would call it — though very little was done to it, by one of my co-editors, the accomplished blind organist, Dr. J. A. [It should be W.] Bischoff, of my church in Washington. I then wrote the other stanzas."

"I have been told," Dr. Rankin said elsewhere, "that it is publicly stated that this hymn was written on the departure of a certain temperance evangelist to Europe. This is wholly a mistake. The above is a complete history of its origin."

And this is from an article Dr. Rankin sent to *The Christian Endeavor World*, in 1894:

"The hymn never was so much used by the First Congregational Church as by all the rest of the world. With the exception of the Sunday night service, it was almost never sung. I think the Methodists at Ocean Grove first began to glorify it. This they carried to such an extent that on the last day of one of their camp meetings a member of my family heard it sung five successive times, as the closing hymn of five different assemblies there." He goes on to speak of his gratification at its adoption by the Christian Endeavor Society.

DR. JEREMIAH EAMES RANKIN

THE AUTHOR OF "GOD BE WITH YOU"

Dr. Rankin did good service in his day, and was regarded by his friends as a man of unusual gifts. He wrote a number of books and became a college president. But to the general public his name survives simply as associated with a single hymn.

The son of a Congregationalist clergyman, he was born on January 2, 1828, in the hamlet of Thornton, that lies by its little river in the hill country of New Hampshire. At twenty he was graduated by Middlebury College, in the neighbor state of Vermont, which afterwards gave him its highest degrees, and chose him to preside over its centennial as a distinguished son. Later in life Dr. Rankin became president of the Howard University in Washington, D. C., founded after the Civil War to help in the higher education of the Negro. He was interested all his life in the advancement of the colored people, and here he spent his last years of active service. Retiring in 1902 to the home of his daughter in Cleveland, there he died on November 28, 1904.

Dr. Rankin had a Scotch pedigree, a great love of Robert Burns, a ready pen of his own, and an early ambition to make his mark in poetry; all of which things showed themselves in his first book, in the Scottish dialect, *Auld Scotch Mither*. Throughout life the writing of verse continued to be his avocation. But his real vocation was in preaching and pastoral work. He served many Congregational churches in New England, New York, and New Jersey. One can picture, above the pulpit, his square face topped with the luxuriant head of dark brown hair, and the piercing eyes underneath the heavy brows, giving it such an intense look. One can almost hear the deep voice speaking rapidly his characteristic short, sharp sentences with all his Scottish fervor and conviction.

The pastorate that concerns us most was at the First Congregational Church of Washington. It was one of those churches started under the conviction that one's own denomination ought to have a representative at the nation's capital; and General Oliver O. Howard, of Civil War fame, traveled all over the country raising money to build it. Dr. Rankin came as pastor in 1869. His fervid preaching at once drew a large congregation, and the evenings gave him opportunity to conduct those informal evangelistic services, for which, as we have seen, his hymn was written.

THE COMPOSER OF THE TUNE

We might indeed say that the composer of the music to " God be with you " was co-author of the hymn itself, for one can hardly think of the words, much less sing them, apart from Mr. Tomer's melody.

William Gould Tomer was not a trained musician. His only education was had at the public school of a hamlet, in Warren County, New Jersey (now known as Finesville). There he was born on October 5, 1833, of Methodist stock, German on his father's side. And there, at the age of seventeen, he ceased to be a scholar in the village school by becoming its teacher. He was a country boy who loved music, who could carry his part in the old-time singing school and lead the village choir on a Sunday. He had taught himself to play the bass viol and violin, and wrote musical sketches that revealed a distinct gift for melody.

The Civil War interrupted his teaching. In 1862 he enlisted as a private and was detailed as clerk to General Howard. On his return home he taught school again, until, in 1865, appointed a clerk in one of the departments at Washington, where he served for some seventeen years.

There Dr. Rankin met him, and formed a pleasant impression of his musical gift. In Washington he did some newspaper work, and in later years was editor of one and another local newspaper in New Jersey towns. At the time of his death, September 26, 1896, in Phillipsburg, where his home was, he was editing *The Hunterdon Gazette*, published in the neighboring High Bridge, New Jersey. And it is a leading article in that newspaper, for October 1, 1896, that has made possible this present sketch of Mr. Tomer's life.

He is described as a figure of five feet ten, of bulky frame, with " a smooth Henry Ward Beecher face, large head, gray eyes and a benign countenance "; an attractive personality, a general utility man with many bents and capacities and a liking to spread his own sunny atmosphere: at his best in his home, where each child could play some musical instrument. Very fitly the choir of the Phillipsburg Methodist Church sang " God be with you " at his funeral; for that is his memorial.

SOME POINTS FOR DISCUSSION

1. Dr. Rankin's hymn does not belong to literature but to the outlying realm of popular song, where the standard is the simpler one of popular effectiveness. It ranges with sentimental songs (most effective songs are sentimental), boating songs, camp-meeting melodies and

" gospel hymns." Dr. Rankin regarded it as a ' gospel hymn,' but in structure and effect it is more like the old Negro ' spirituals ' (" Swing low, sweet chariot," for instance), that take a melodious phrase for a theme, repeat it, play around it, and come back to it with brief intervals.

As sung there are thirty-two lines in all. Of these just twelve are the first line over and over again, and in twelve other lines " till we meet " is read twenty times and sung forty times. Only eight lines are left in which to add any thoughts to the original theme, and most of these are turned from very familiar Scripture phrases. So commonplace are they indeed that one might almost say the hymn contains hardly more than the melodious first line itself.

In song, as we all know, the recurrence of the main theme as a refrain is an old and effective device. But a case so extreme as this seems to invite criticism; and first, from the artistic point of view. Even the simplest art should " hold, as 't were, the mirror up to nature," and in our human intercourse such a prolongation and repetition of " Good bye " would be as unnatural as unwelcome. Secondly, it invites criticism from a spiritual point of view, for the hymn is throughout a prayer; and in prayer we are forbidden to employ " vain repetitions." Which probably means that we must not repeat phrases mechanically without attending to what we say, or imagine that petitions, if repeated many times, are more effective than if said only once.

The repetitions of the present hymn have not in actual experience interfered with the powerful emotional appeal it has made to a vast company of Christians: they have probably consolidated it by diverting the singers from the necessity of doing any thinking or even much remembering. Wherein does the power of that emotional appeal lie?

First, in the simple words "Good bye," which the opening line draws out so melodiously and the added lines perhaps amplify. As Mark Rutherford says in his novel, *Catharine Furze,* "In all parting there is something infinite."

Second, in Mr. Tomer's music, which has the half-pathetic strain loved by young people in their college and other songs. In its way the music is quite remarkable in suggesting the bright hopes and vague shadows that lurk around "good-bye." Whether into the dark or into the light, it's "God be with you" where we cannot go! And so the melody flows on and turns back; now loud and clear at the doorway where we separate, now lessening with the lengthening roads that bear us apart, now as a last refrain, so faint, so far, and, then, remembered music.

2. Dr. Rankin was somewhat vehement in protesting against any alteration of his hymn. One "tinker," he said, printed "Put His loving arms around you" in place of "Put His arms unfailing round you": "an idea unpleasant and out of taste, besides being unscriptural: as in the Bible the arms always signify strength, especially when applied to Jehovah." Is he right as to the Biblical usage?

Another "tinker" printed "still provide you" in place of "still divide you," intended to suggest Christ's breaking and distribution of bread. This tinker, Dr. Rankin said, might have served as a butler or commissary.

3. When in 1889 Dr. Rankin printed his *Hymns pro*

Patria, he doubled the length of this, adding four verses. Could there have been a call for forty additional repeats of " Till we meet " ? And was there no kindly hand raised to prevent the printing of this final verse?

> " God be with you till we meet again,
> Ended when for you earth's story,
> Israel's chariot sweep to glory:
> God be with you till we meet again."

4. In concluding these studies of hymn origins, the writer wonders how many readers have come so far with him, and if any has learned to turn a more interested eye on his church hymnal; and especially if he has yet begun to notice the inconspicuous note to each hymn and tune that discloses its authorship and date, and the state of the hymn's text. The writer would like to tell the story of all that was involved in preparing the notes to this hymn and tune as one illustration of the painstaking that goes into a good hymnal. For the sake of directness he will tell it in the first person.

When I wrote Dr. Rankin for permission to use words and music in *The Hymnal* of 1895, I asked for the correct date of each. He replied that he could not tell " without great inconvenience and loss of time." He did not even know Mr. Tomer's full name or address. So both hymn and tune went in without a date. Soon after I secured for the tune a date I thought trustworthy (as it was) ; and so in the second edition it was dated 1880. In correcting the plates for a fourth printing this date was struck out through some misunderstanding, and hymn and tune appeared once more without any date. Then I came upon a quotation from a letter of Dr. Rankin, saying that both were written in 1882. Supposing he had looked up the matter at last, that date was given to both words and music in the edition of *The Hymnal* printed in 1899, and was kept when *The Hymnal revised* was published in 1911, and printed there till now.

One day in May, 1921, I was looking over a poor lot of old ' gospel ' song books in Highlands' second-hand book store on Arch Street, Philadelphia, and came upon one called *Gospel Bells*. Its editors were named as " Prof. J. W. Bischoff, Otis F. Presbrey and Rev. J. E. Rankin, D.D.," and it was published in Chicago, 1880. Here plainly was the song book that Dr. Rankin and his blind organist prepared for the evangelistic services at Washington, and here, surely enough, was " God be with you," on page 51, words and music, just as it is sung now. Sometimes these books are dated ahead, for reasons publishers know. But this particular copy has a penciled note stating that it was bought " Nov. 1880." So we have at last the correct date of the first printing of our hymn and tune. And the Hymnal plates will have to be altered once more.

GENERAL INDEX

[Titles of books, etc., in Italics.]

INDEX OF FIRST LINES OF HYMNS

[*Those which are the subjects of the Studies are printed in Italics.*]

50